This book is dedicated to the uncounted people all over the world who have been affected by AIDS; to those who have died or who have grieved for their dead; to those who have been blamed, stigmatised or persecuted as a result of having AIDS or being HIV positive; to those who have been labelled as "high risk" persons. The book has been written in the knowledge that many more people are likely to suffer the double oppression of AIDS and of discrimination, and in the hope that it may help to reduce their burden.

BLAMING OTHERS
Prejudice, race and worldwide AIDS

by

Renée Sabatier

with contributions from
Tade Aina, Patricia Ardila, Erlinda Bolido, Philippe
Engelhard, K.S. Jayaraman, Dave Moyo, Dorothy
Kweyu Munyakho, Hikloch Ogola, Seun Ogunseitan,
Abib Samb, Moussa Seck, Lazaro Timmo and others.

research by
Martin Foreman and Marty Radlett

edited by
Jon Tinker

The Panos Institute
London — Paris —Washington

Published by Panos Publications Ltd
9 White Lion Street
London N1 9PD, UK

First published 1988
Reprinted 1990

British Library Cataloguing-in-Publication data:
Blaming Others: prejudice, race and worldwide AIDS
1. Man. AIDS. Social aspects
I. Sabatier, Renée
362.1'042

ISBN 1-870670-03-5

The work of the Panos AIDS Unit is supported financially by the
Norwegian Ministry for Development Cooperation and the Norwegian Red
Cross. Funds toward the publication of *Blaming Others* were given by the
Swedish Red Cross. Additional financial assistance was provided by Save
the Children; Memisa Medicus Mundi (Netherlands); Rädda Barnen (Save
the Children, Sweden); Oxfam (UK); Christian Aid (UK) and Action Aid.

Any judgements expressed in this document should not be taken to
represent the view of any funding agency.

The Panos Institute is an international information and policy studies
institute, dedicated to working in partnership with others towards greater
public understanding of sustainable development. Panos has offices in
London, Paris and Washington DC, and was founded in 1986 by the staff of
Earthscan, which has undertaken similar work since 1975.

For more information about Panos contact:
James Deane, The Panos Institute.

Produced by Jacqueline Walkden and Gillian Hitchcock
Photo research: Patricia Lee
Cover design: Robert Purnell
Graphs: Philip Davies

Printed in Great Britain by BPCC Wheatons Ltd, Exeter

CONTENTS

ACKNOWLEDGEMENTS

Blaming Others was written by Renée Sabatier and edited by Jon Tinker, who are respectively the AIDS Unit director and the president of the Panos Institute.

Extensive research, interviewing, and co-ordinating of the work on this book was performed by Panos AIDS Unit staff members Martin Foreman and Marty Radlett.

Several people with AIDS (PWAs) generously gave of their time and experience during the research for this book. Those whose stories appear in it are Richard Rector, "Lisa", and "Geraldo". The Reverend Charles Angel, who gave advice during what was to be his final bout of illness, died of AIDS in New York City before his contributed article was completed. Sam Akinlade, executive officer of the National Union of Students, London, shared his insights freely, and died by his own hand before the book was published.

Many Panos staff members, especially Patricia Ardila and Rosemarie Philips in Washington, contributed other useful material.

Many other individuals and organisations, both in developing and developed countries, made valuable contributions to the book at various stages. Space prevents thanking them all, but a list of those who read and commented on drafts or chapters of the book, or who were interviewed, or who provided documents or other information appears after the concluding chapter. These people, and the members of the advisory panel named below, have made this book possible; but they do not necessarily endorse everything in it.

The Panos AIDS Unit thanks the members of its expert advisory panel for their invaluable advice, assistance and support. Most of their comments and suggestions on previous drafts of this book have been incorporated in the final version.

ADVISORY PANEL

Calle Almedal, Nordic Red Cross AIDS Coordinator, Norwegian Red Cross, Oslo, Norway.

Dr Jonathan Mann, Director, Global Programme on AIDS, WHO, Geneva.

Dr Jean William Pape, Assistant Professor of Medicine, Cornell University Medical College and State University of Haiti (Port au Prince).

Dr Anthony Pinching, Consultant Immunologist, St Mary's Hospital, London, UK

Dr Peter Piot, Head, Department of Microbiology, Institute of Tropical Medicine, Antwerp, Belgium.

Dr Pramilla Senanayake, Assistant Secretary General, technical services, International Planned Parenthood Federation, London, UK.

Dr Richard Tedder, Head, Department of Virology, Middlesex Hospital Medical School, London, UK.

CHAPTER ONE

AIDS AND RACE: WHY IT MATTERS

AIDS is overwhelmingly a sexually transmitted disease, although the virus which causes it can also be transferred through contaminated blood and from mother to child before, during, and possibly after birth.

We have as yet no vaccine to protect ourselves against HIV*, and there is no effective treatment for the illness once it develops. Although some therapies can slow down the process, people with AIDS usually die within a few years of developing symptoms.

The vast majority of people with AIDS have been infected during sexual activity with another HIV-carrier. The most important weapon we have against AIDS, therefore, is to reduce further sexual transmission of the virus; this is done either through safer sex or through reducing the number of sexual partners per person.

To understand how HIV spreads we need to know much more about sexual habits in different countries and communities. And the best way to slow the momentum of the virus in the community is sex education: persuading people to change the sexual habits which place them at risk.

But sex in nearly all human societies is surrounded by taboos. Few people discuss such a sensitive issue without making or implying moral judgements — or feeling that moral judgements are being made about them. And when people from one ethnic group discuss AIDS in another ethnic group, which inevitably involves discussing other people's sexual behaviour, suspicions of racial and ethnic prejudice are easily aroused.

This would be easier to handle if AIDS were affecting all nations and ethnic communities equally, but this is not the case. AIDS was first noticed as an epidemic among homosexual men in North America and Europe. Since then, major epidemics have been detected in the Caribbean, Africa and other parts of the Third World — and in the black and hispanic ethnic minorities in the United States. Indeed, the epidemics among people of colour often seem, in per capita terms, to be worse than among people of north European descent.

---

* The human immunodeficiency virus, identified as the cause of AIDS, and formerly known as HTLV-3 in the United States and LAV (in France). HIV is now the internationally-agreed term.

Discussions about whether this is the case, and if so why, have become complicated by racial prejudices — real and perceived. They have also been complicated, in the early stages of the epidemics, by the denial by the communities affected that the problem existed at all. This denial is a near universal response to the fact of AIDS, obscuring facts, complicating issues, and delaying preventive action. In each country and group affected by AIDS denial has made it more difficult to coolly and calmly examine the economic, cultural, behavioural and other patterns which help to render people more vulnerable to the virus and which, once recognised as damaging, are amenable to change. Instead of recognising these patterns for the malleable human artefacts they are, the tendency has been to label the people affected by AIDS according to their sexual, socio-economic, racial or ethnic group, a tendency which has repeatedly interfered with the battle against the disease.

Other key elements of the AIDS debate have a similar capacity for arousing inter-racial tensions. Where did the disease first originate? Are some racial groups more susceptible to it than others? Should countries screen foreign tourists, or businessmen, or students, to prevent the entry of HIV-infected people? What is the role of other sexually-transmitted diseases (such as genital ulcers and chlamydia) in helping the spread of AIDS? Why should AIDS be predominantly homosexually-transmitted in Europe and predominantly heterosexually-transmitted in Africa? What is the role of prostitutes in different societies? How many sexual partners do people have, and how does this vary from one community to another?

These issues are all more or less important, and have to be discussed if the AIDS pandemic is to be fought. But all these issues have acquired moral overtones, of which the main one is the question of *blame*.

THE THIRD EPIDEMIC

Blaming other people for a problem, as a substitute for tackling the problem itself, is a very human characteristic. Societies are especially liable to blame other people when misfortunes seem inexplicable or outside their control — something that applies particularly to AIDS.

The process of attributing blame does not always require evidence, and tends to focus on people who are not considered normal by the majority, especially minorities or foreigners. Epidemics of dangerous infections such as plague, smallpox, syphilis or even influenza have historically prompted social responses based on blaming others for spreading the disease by their "deviant" behaviour. Blaming others may itself be a contagious psychological process, leading on to stigmatisation, scapegoating and persecution.[1]

2

When whole communities blame others for a problem, the results can be traumatic. While the Black Death, an epidemic of bubonic plague, swept across Europe in the fourteenth century, blame was variously attached to Jews and witches, followed by massacres and burnings of the alleged culprits. And when Hitler blamed Jews, communists, homosexuals and other "undesireables" for the economic stagnation of Germany in the 1920s, the result was death camps and European war.

Dr Jonathan Mann, who heads the World Health Organization's global programme on AIDS, points out that there are really *three* AIDS epidemics, which are in fact phases in the invasion of a community by the AIDS virus. Each community attacked by AIDS suffers the three phases consecutively.

The first is the epidemic of silent infection by the HIV virus, often completely unnoticed.

The second, after a delay of several years, is the epidemic of the disease AIDS itself, of which more than 85,000 cases had been reported worldwide by March 1988.

*This British headline (left: **Daily Telegraph**, 20 September 1986) was followed by story calling for blood tests for all visitors, especially students, from three African countries, and led to Zambia retarding co-operation with British AIDS experts. The other headline (right: **Kenya Times**, 4 December 1986) introduced a story arguing that Panos, among others, was giving misleading information on AIDS in Africa.*

The third is the epidemic of social, cultural, economic and political reactions to AIDS, which is also worldwide, and "as central to the global AIDS challenge as the disease itself". [2]

This book discusses one aspect of that third epidemic. It looks at the explosions of accusation and blame which are following the advance of the AIDS virus across the globe. AIDS is variously blamed on homosexual men, on drug addicts, on ethnic minorities, on Haitians, on foreign students, on US tourists, on Africans, on prostitutes, on US seamen, on Western scientists. The aim of the book is not to criticise, but rather to show the dangers of blaming as a reaction to AIDS: not only does it blur the vision of the "blamer", but it endangers those who are singled out for blame, all the while inhibiting AIDS prevention.

AIDS outside the United States and Europe, particularly in Haiti and Africa, has received a great deal of media coverage. Some of this press attention has been seen in the Third World as too clouded by Western preconceptions to portray the impact of the epidemic accurately. Some Third Worlders believe that this media coverage has caused Western scientists and journalists to exaggerate and mischaracterise AIDS in Africa. Anger, resentment, confusion, weariness and demoralisation have resulted, eating up precious time and deflecting vital energies from the battle against the virus. Bitterness over this racial aspect of AIDS has led some Africans and minority groups to deny that AIDS exists in their communities.

Once the AIDS virus has entered a society, it tends towards the path of least resistance. Globally, that line runs directly through some of the world's least powerful communities: the poorest, most disadvantaged and underdeveloped groups whose members constitute an increasingly disproportionate share of the world's total AIDS cases. This includes communities in the Third World and also impoverished ethnic minorities, often of Third World descent, within some developed nations.

Worldwide, close to half the people who have already developed AIDS are people of colour, a proportion which seems likely to rise steadily over the coming years. A similar percentage of the estimated one million people[3] who are likely to develop AIDS in the next three years will come from the Third World. They already carry HIV, most of them unknowingly.

They are, without being aware of it, passing the virus to yet another tier of people who lack the only form of protection yet devised against it: information. For many people in the Third World, this lack of knowledge about the AIDS virus and how it spreads is but the most recent of the many forms of life-threatening disadvantage that they already face.

AIDS is in reality the latest trend to emerge beside all those other epidemics — of infant mortality and malnutrition, of sexually transmitted and other infectious diseases, of heart disease, stroke and diabetes, of alcohol and drug misuse and of psychological distress and social disruption — which disproportionately affect the globally disadvantaged. The AIDS pandemic cannot be properly understood apart from this background, and it is arguable that AIDS will never be controlled, let alone eliminated, without a change in the combined conditions of underdevelopment, unbalanced development and the economic and political marginalisation which provide it with such fertile soil.

Blaming Others examines how racial and ethnic aspects of AIDS have affected the course of the pandemic so far. Important parts of the book have been written by journalists and researchers from Africa, Latin America and Asia, and from US ethnic minority communities.

Blaming Others recognises that many aspects of AIDS are racially and ethnically sensitive, so much so that individuals and governments sometimes respond to factual discussion as if it implied moral judgements against groups of people or whole communities. Sometimes discussion *is* motivated by deliberate racism, or by inbuilt prejudices of which the speaker is unaware. And sometimes a listener reads moral criticism or condemnation into humanitarian concern.

An earlier publication of the Panos Institute, *AIDS and the Third World*, published in November 1986, played an important part in alerting world opinion to the growing dangers of the AIDS pandemic. Although it has been adapted and translated in many countries, and been used by many Third World governments and institutions, it has also been criticised. Some of these criticisms are discussed in *Blaming Others*.

It would be foolish to follow the present epidemic of blaming others with an analysis of who is to blame for casting blame. So this book endeavours to be scrupulously non-judgmental. Readers must judge for themselves where blame has been maliciously, carelessly or deliberately implied, or where people have dismissed comments as racist when no such slur was intended, or where the charge of racial prejudice has been a convenient tool to avoid discussing the real dangers of AIDS.

AIDS seems likely to be a dominating component of international relations for many years to come. This will involve a continuing debate on the sexual behaviour of others. It would be irresponsible to allow this discussion to be stifled by the sensitivities which surround sex. Equally, we all have an obligation to avoid giving unnecessary offence to others.

Chapter Two of this book, "A Disease of Disadvantage", describes the vulnerability to AIDS of people in globally disadvantaged groups: in ethnic minorities in the United States, and in various parts of the Third World.

Chapter Three, "Portraits of Vulnerability", describes a series of such groups, either already badly affected by AIDS or on the verge of becoming so.

Chapter Four, "Origins of AIDS, Origins of Blame", looks at the possible origins of the AIDS epidemic, an issue which is central to the epidemic of blame. It examines the evidence for HIV having started in Haiti or in Africa, and looks back to the notional "first case" of AIDS.

Chapter Five, "Green Monkeys and Germ Warfare", considers the possibilities that the AIDS virus has evolved from an animal infection or that it is a virus manufactured in a military laboratory. Both theories have led to irrational episodes of blaming others.

Chapter Six, "Sex and Race", discusses the spread of HIV, and factors which may influence it: the role of other sexually-transmitted diseases (genital ulcers and chlamydia, for example), the degree of sexual partner-change ("promiscuity") in various societies, and the possibility that some ethnic groups might be genetically more or less susceptible to the AIDS virus.

Chapter Seven, "Blame and Counter-blame", looks at Western responses to AIDS in Africa, and African reactions to these views, especially in the media. Drawing heavily on the views of Third World authors, it describes how dangerously infectious the phenomenon of blaming has been.

Chapter Eight, "Who Pays the Price of Blame?", describes how African students in India and Europe, and the Kenyan tourist industry, have been harmed by blame for AIDS. It looks at actions against AIDS taken by various governments worldwide, and suggests that many such measures have been influenced as much by the wish to blame outsiders as by rational public health considerations.

Chapter Nine, "Different Peoples, Different Messages", describes how a number of Third World societies, and some ethnic minority communities in the United States and elsewhere, are tackling AIDS education.

Finally, **Chapter Ten**, "Conclusions", argues that it is more accurate to talk about "risk activities" rather than "risk groups". It suggests that AIDS may have one benefit if it focuses sustained attention and action on the causes of disadvantage which makes some communities more vulnerable to AIDS than others.

CHAPTER TWO

A DISEASE OF DISADVANTAGE

AIDS is still widely regarded as a disease which primarily affects homosexual white men in the United States. This picture is no longer true internationally — nor is it true in the United States itself. Of all reported US AIDS cases, almost 40% occur in people of black or hispanic origin, although these groups comprise only 19% of the US population.

Seven years into the AIDS epidemic in the United States, it is becoming clear that what was originally perceived as a disease of white middle-class homosexuals has also been the unnoticed tragedy of the minorities, the disadvantaged, and the disenfranchised.

AIDS HITS US BLACKS AND HISPANICS

Among white adults in the United States, the incidence of AIDS cases is 189 per million population; for blacks it is 578 per million; and for hispanics it is 564 per million. Other ethnic minorities in the United States, by contrast, to date appear less affected than whites by HIV infection and AIDS: the remaining population, which includes Asian Americans and Native Americans, has only 74 adult cases per million.[1] It is possible, however, that this lower incidence of AIDS merely reflects the later entry of the virus into Asian and native American groups.

These figures mean that a black or hispanic person in the United States is three times more likely to have AIDS than a white. And while the rate at which new cases of AIDS are being reported in white adults, and among homosexual men, is slowing a little, the reporting rate for black and hispanic adults is accelerating, (see Figure 2.1).

Women of colour in the United States are even more vulnerable than men. Black and hispanic women account for 71% of all women with AIDS. A black women is 13 times more likely to have AIDS than her white counterpart; an hispanic woman is 9 times more likely.[2]

The US secretary of health and human resources concluded in early 1988 that the heterosexual spread of HIV was not on the rise overall in the United States.[3] But among blacks and hispanics, heterosexual spread is undeniably a major factor. Among whites with AIDS, only about 1% are thought to have contracted the virus through heterosexual contact. For hispanics the comparable figure is 4%, and for blacks it is 11%.

The inevitable consequence of the heterosexual transmission of HIV is that babies will be born carrying the AIDS virus, and that many infants will develop AIDS. This is already a growing problem for these US ethnic minorities. Of all US children with AIDS, 77% are black or hispanic. The New York State Public Health Department estimates that 1,000 HIV-infected babies will be born in 1988[4]; nationwide, the estimate ranges from 1,620 to 4,860.[5] Black babies are 16 times, and hispanic babies 11 times, more likely to have AIDS than are white infants.

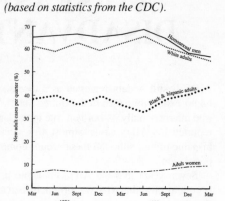

Figure 2.1: New US AIDS cases by race and sex (based on statistics from the CDC).

In a 1987 blood survey of pregnant women in New York City, 1.64% of the women were seropositive for HIV.[6] This figure is comparable to that found among women at antenatal clinics in Nairobi, among women in rural Haiti[7], and among the general population of several Central African countries.[8] Women and children are the fastest growing categories of AIDS patients in New York, with 84% of female cases now occurring among minority women. AIDS is now the single biggest cause of death for women of all races between the ages of 25-34 in New York City; the same has been true for men of this age-group for several years.[9]

By 1991, the United States expects to have a total of 270,000 cases of AIDS. If present trends continue, 108,000 of these will be among New York blacks and hispanics, most of them occurring in low income inner city areas.

Although the best statistics come from New York, other big US cities have similar problems. During 1985/6, testing of blood donors in Atlanta, Baltimore and Los Angeles showed blacks to be over 15 times more likely to carry HIV than whites, with hispanics four times more likely.[10] Nationwide, the picture is similar; blood surveys of military volunteers show that blacks are four times, and hispanics two times, more likely than whites to carry the AIDS virus.[11]

8

WHY ARE US ETHNIC MINORITIES BEING HIT SO HARD?

The idea that the nation is a great melting pot of immigrants is one of the United States' most cherished beliefs. In reality, not all that goes into the pot melts. Nor do all ethnic minorities receive their fair share of the benefits which balance the costs of assimilation.

AIDS is not the only disease which disproportionately hits minorities in the United States. Their health compares poorly to that of whites in many other ways. The six major causes of death in the United States are heart disease and stroke, homicide and accidents, cancer, cirrhosis, diabetes and infant mortality. From all these causes, according to a United States Government report, blacks are more likely to die than whites.[12] Blacks and other US ethnic minorities not only suffer disproportionately from conditions such as excess infant mortality, which are clearly related to poverty and deprivation, but also from many of the causes of death associated with advanced industrial societies. AIDS is only the most recent of many epidemics which strike disproportionately at the most vulnerable groups within US society: epidemics which can and have been controlled among more privileged groups.

The AIDS Discrimination Unit of the New York City Commission on Human Rights stated in 1987 that "it is behaviour and not one's race or ethnicity that is the operative risk factor" with most modes of HIV transmission.[13] Obvious though this remark sounds, it took two years for the US Centers for Disease Control to stop referring to Haitians — as a nationality — as a "high risk group" for AIDS (see Chapter Three). And only very recently have some officials in US federal, state and local health agencies begun to talk about "high risk behaviour" rather than "high risk groups".

The inadequate official response to the danger which US ethnic minorities are facing from AIDS will be covered in more detail in Chapter Eight. "This disease is becoming the particular scourge of people who are young, black and hispanic", US surgeon general, C. Everett Koop, said in September 1987. "How tragic that is for them, but also, how tragic it is for America....This country is only now emerging from two decades of turmoil during which we have tried to correct the injustices of the past. Now, will the disease AIDS, by itself, reverse this trend of history?"[14]

THE GLOBAL AIDS PATTERN

There is no doubt that the United States has one of the most severe AIDS epidemics in the world. But, although in early 1988 the United States had 65% of all the AIDS cases reported to the World Health

Organization, a number of Third World countries are, in per capita terms, considerably worse off.

Figure 2.2 shows the 10 countries most affected by AIDS epidemics, in terms of cumulative cases reported to the World Health Organization (WHO) per million population. These figures should be read with caution, especially those from countries with less than a million population, where a few cases can disproportionately affect the per capita total. Moreover, the number of cases in smaller countries may include a higher percentage among people who contracted it abroad and then returned home. The figures may also be misleading in that in the United States and in some African countries, AIDS cases are heavily concentrated in major cities, and not spread throughout rural areas.

Figure 2.2: COUNTRIES MOST AFFECTED BY AIDS IN TERMS OF REPORTED CASES PER CAPITA

	Officially reported cases	National population	AIDS cases per million population
Bermuda	75	56,000	1339
French Guiana	93	82,000	1134
Bahamas	163	235,000	694
Congo	1,250	2,100,000	595
USA	57,024	243,800,000	234
Guadeloupe	61	300,000	203
Burundi	960	5,000,000	192
Haiti	1,155	6,200,000	186
Barbados	52	300,000	173
Trinidad	206	1,300,000	158

Source: Panos, based on Ministry of Health and WHO's figures officially reported by March 1988, excluding countries reporting fewer than 10 cases.

Nevertheless, it is clear that in per capita terms a number of Third World countries already have statistically more severe AIDS epidemics than does the United States.

Figure 2.3 shows similar figures from all over the world, again as reported by March 1988. In all, six countries, including the United States, have reported over 200 cases per million population. Five of those six are in the Third World — the Congo in Africa and the small Caribbean nations of Bermuda, French Guiana, Bahamas and Guadeloupe.

A further seven countries, all but one in the Third World, have reported over 100 cases per million: Burundi, Haiti, Barbados, Trinidad, Uganda, Rwanda and Qatar. And another 11 countries have reported 50-100 cases of AIDS per million (under half the US level): Canada, Central African Republic, Malawi, Zambia, Tanzania, Kenya, Martinique, Netherlands Antilles, Dominican Republic, France and Switzerland.

Figure 2.3: NATIONAL AIDS EPIDEMICS at March 1988

	Officially reported cases	National population	AIDS cases per million population
AFRICA			
Congo	1,250	2,100,000	595
Burundi	960	5,000,000	192
Uganda	2,369	15,900,000	149
Rwanda	901	6,800,000	133
Central Afr Rep	254	2,700,000	94
Malawi	583	7,400,000	79
Zambia	536	7,100,000	75
Tanzania	1,608	23,500,000	68
Kenya	1,304	22,400,000	58
Zimbabwe	380	9,400,000	40
Gambia	27	800,000	34
Ivory Coast	250	10,800,000	23
Guinea-Bissau	16	900,000	18
Botswana	16	1,200,000	13
Gabon	13	1,150,000	11
Zaire	335	31,800,000	11
Ghana	145	13,900,000	10
Senegal	66	7,100,000	9
Cameroon	47	10,300,000	5
Burkina Faso	26	7,300,000	4
Mali	29	8,400,000	3
Angola	23	8,000,000	3
South Africa	98	34,300,000	3
Tunisia	19	7,600,000	3
Sudan	35	23,500,000	1
Ethiopia	19	46,000,000	0.4
CARIBBEAN			
Bermuda	75	56,000	1339
Bahamas	163	235,000	694
Guadeloupe	61	300,000	203
Haiti	1,155	6,200,000	186
Barbados	52	300,000	173
Trinidad	206	1,300,000	158
Martinique	27	300,000	90
Neth Antilles	18	200,000	90
Dominican Rep	400	6,500,000	62
Jamaica	44	2,500,000	18
Cuba	27	10,300,000	3

LATIN AMERICA

French Guiana	93	82,000	1134
Brazil	2,458	141,500,000	17
Honduras	81	4,700,000	17
Mexico	1,200	81,900,000	15
Costa Rica	39	2,800,000	14
Panama	27	2,300,000	12
Venezuela	101	18,300,000	5
Nicaragua	19	3,500,000	5
Ecuador	52	10,000,000	5
Uruguay	16	3,100,000	5
Colombia	153	29,900,000	5
El Salvador	25	5,300,000	5
Chile	56	12,400,000	5
Argentina	120	31,500,000	4
Guatemala	30	8,400,000	4
Paraguay	14	4,300,000	3
Peru	44	20,700,000	2

NORTH AMERICA

USA	57,024	243,800,000	234
Canada	1,608	25,900,000	62

ASIA

Qatar	32	300,000	107
Israel	47	4,400,000	11
Japan	66	122,000,000	0.5
Turkey	25	51,400,000	0.5
Thailand	12	53,600,000	0.2
Philippines	11	61,500,000	0.2

EUROPE

France	3,073	55,600,000	55
Switzerland	355	6,600,000	54
Denmark	228	5,100,000	45
West Germany	1,848	61,000,000	30
Belgium	297	9,900,000	30
Netherlands	420	14,600,000	29
Italy	1,619	57,400,000	28
UK	1,344	56,800,000	24
Sweden	174	8,400,000	21
Spain	789	39,000,000	20
Austria	151	7,600,000	20
Norway	75	4,200,000	18
Ireland	33	3,500,000	9
Greece	88	10,000,000	9
Portugal	90	10,300,000	9
Finland	24	4,900,000	5
Yugoslavia	26	23,400,000	1
Hungary	11	10,600,000	1

OCEANIA

Australia	758	16,200,000	47
New Zealand	74	3,300,000	22

Source: Panos, based on Ministry of Health and WHO's figures officially reported by March 1988, excluding countries reporting fewer than 10 cases.

The 40-50 cases per million group (under one quarter the US level) consists of Denmark, Australia and Zimbabwe. And in the 10-40 cases per million group we find seven African countries (Gambia, Ivory Coast, Guinea-Bissau, Botswana, Gabon, Zaire and Ghana); one Caribbean country (Jamaica); five Latin American countries (Brazil, Honduras, Mexico, Costa Rica and Panama); and 11 European or other developed countries (West Germany, Belgium, The Netherlands, Italy, United Kingdom, New Zealand, Sweden, Spain, Austria, Norway and Israel) — a total of 13 Third World and 11 developed countries.

So far, South American countries (other than French Guiana and Brazil) have under 10 cases per million, and other than Qatar and Israel all Asian countries have well below one case per million.

WHAT DO THE FIGURES MEAN?

Globally, then, AIDS epidemics appear to be most serious in Africa, the Caribbean, Europe and North America — with 17 of the top 19 countries from Africa and the Caribbean.

But there are a variety of logistical, economic and political reasons for supposing that official figures, especially those from the Third World, significantly underestimate the real position.

A few countries do not report AIDS cases at all, although the number of non-reporting countries decreased dramatically during 1987 and early 1988. In the United States, analyses suggest that about 90% of the AIDS cases meeting the official WHO criteria are actually reported.[15] Across Europe as many as 50% of cases may go unreported.[16] In developing countries, where medical surveillance systems are usually weaker, far more AIDS cases are not reported to the national health authorities.

WHO estimates that, worldwide to the end of 1987, only about half of all AIDS cases had been reported to it. Pan American Health Organization officials estimate that in Latin America 10-50% of AIDS cases are not reported.[17]

According to WHO and other authorities, "reporting of AIDS cases in Africa has in general been delayed or incomplete", due to "limited access of large segments of the population to health care facilities where the diagnosis of AIDS can be established, the low efficiency of surveillance systems, the general lack of facilities for the diagnosis of AIDS, and the reluctance of some governments to acknowledge the existence of AIDS until 1987".[18] AIDS statistics, particularly in Africa, where the false results of early blood test surveys have muddied the waters (see Chapter Four), remain an extremely sensitive issue politically, as do claims made by Westerners that rates of under-reporting on the continent are high.

13

THE COSTS TO THE THIRD WORLD

AIDS is an expensive illness, and the true extent of its impact depends on the resources a nation can make available for treatment, prevention, education and research. Even taking into account its large number of AIDS cases, the United States is in a strong economic position to combat its AIDS epidemic.

In many AIDS-affected countries in Africa, annual per capita health spending is less than the cost of a single HIV blood test. The disproportion between per capita AIDS cases and per capita income (gross national product per person) in developing countries is shown in Figure 2.4. Column one shows each country's AIDS epidemic as a percentage of the US epidemic, measured in cases per million population. Column two shows national per capita income, again expressed as a percentage of US per capita income.

Figure 2.4: AIDS RESOURCES INDEX

Country	AIDS epidemic	Per capita income	AIDS resources index
Sweden	9 %	71%	755%
Switzerland	23	98	427
Mexico	4	12	272
France	23	57	248
Brazil	8	10	120
USA	100	100	100
Honduras	5	4	73
Trinidad	80	36	45
Zimbabwe	20	4	20
Zaire	5	1	19
Dominican Rep	27	5	18
Kenya	22	2	9
Zambia	38	2	5
Rwanda	53	2	4
Haiti	74	2	3
Uganda	75	1	1

Column one shows cases of AIDS per million population as a percentage of the US total per million (based on WHO statistics as of December 1987).
Column two shows GNP per capita as a percentage of the US GNP per capita (source: World Bank 1987).
Column three is column two divided by column one, expressed as a percentage.

Column three shows an AIDS Resources Index: column two as a percentage of column one. This is a crude estimation of the resources a country can make available for combating its AIDS epidemic.

With all its limitations, the table makes some interesting points. Sweden and Switzerland and France have roughly two to eight times more economic resources available per case of AIDS than does the United States, and Mexico has three times more.

At the bottom end of the table, Zambia, Rwanda, Haiti and Uganda are already finding AIDS from 20-100 times more of an economic burden than in the United States.

THE DEVELOPMENT IMPACT OF AIDS

The AIDS epidemic is not just an economic burden. It affects, in terms of social and economic development, the most vital segment of the population — adults 20-49 years old. Though the virus itself does not discriminate between black or white, rich or poor, the loss of these young adults in Third World communities can be disproportionately damaging.

Fewer Third World teenagers have opportunities for higher education than those in developed countries, and when educated people in the 20-49 age group die, they are much less easily replaced. Dr Jonathan Mann, head of WHO's global programme on AIDS, warns of the "potential for economic and political destabilisation in areas of the developing world most affected by HIV. What political system could withstand the ultimate destabilising impact of a 20% or 25% or higher infection rate among young adults?"[19]

In urban areas in some sub-Saharan countries, up to 25% of young adults are *already* HIV carriers, with rates among those reporting to clinics for sexually transmitted diseases passing 30%, and among female prostitutes up to 90%.[20]

The annual incidence of AIDS among adults in Kinshasa, Zaire, has been estimated at 55-100 cases of AIDS per 100,000 population.[21] By comparison, in New York City, the annual incidence in adults in 1986 was 110 per 100,000 for men and 12 per 100,000 for women.[22]

New York City's epidemic is thus roughly comparable in size with that of Kinshasa, but New York's financial and medical resources are many times greater. The whole of Zaire depends on one large teaching hospital in Kinshasa as a centre for both treatment and medical expertise, while New York has dozens of comparable facilities. And whereas Kinshasa is the political, economic, commercial, military and transport heart of Zaire, New York is but one of many equivalent centres in the United States. New York also benefits from US federal government funding for AIDS research and treatment, which is targeted to exceed US$1 billion for 1989, a sum three times greater than the total annual foreign assistance from all sources received by Zaire in 1987.

In some central African hospitals a quarter to a third of scarce hospital beds are occupied by AIDS patients,[23] while even in less heavily-affected Costa Rica officials have predicted that a similar percentage of beds could be taken by AIDS patients by the mid-1990s.[24]

In the cities of several central African countries, 5-25% of women in their childbearing years have been found to be HIV- positive.[25] The transmission of HIV from infected mothers to their infants means that, like New York, African cities face a rapidly growing epidemic of HIV and AIDS in children. Infant mortality rates in parts of Africa, although among the highest in the world, have been slowly but fairly steadily declining over the past decade. AIDS could wipe out these hard-won gains[26] to the point where infant mortality from AIDS alone may exceed the infant mortality rate from all causes in industrialised countries.[27]

Though it cannot yet be forecast accurately, the impact of AIDS on social and economic development in the Third World may be critical. "AIDS may cause mortality rates among the economically and socially most productive age groups to double, triple, or rise even higher", Mann adds.[28] Some African countries are facing the possibility that, in certain regions, negative population growth may occur within several decades.[29]

What will be the general economic effects in the Third World of premature deaths due to AIDS? Prediction is difficult due to lack of basic data, but a preliminary study by Harvard University showed that economic losses due to AIDS in five seriously- affected central African countries could begin to exceed total foreign aid to those countries by 1991.[30]

In some countries key industries may be jeopardised. Zambia's copperbelt, a region that produces 20% of Zambia's gross national product with just 6% of its labour force, faces labour losses due to AIDS which Zambian researchers believe could damage the viability of the whole mining industry.[31] Such national economic losses are accompanied by hardship on a human scale. In a number of African cultures mourning takes the form of lengthy funeral ceremonies which numerous family members gather to attend. A Zairean family, one of whose children has died of AIDS, may spend up to the equivalent of a year's income on the funeral and interment.[32]

Such an impact could not come at a worse time. Both national and per capita incomes in many African countries have been falling for several years, with the economies of some countries, like Zambia, contracting by nearly half. As a continent, Africa is staggering under a foreign debt load described by UN Secretary-General Javier Perez

16

de Cuellar as "the most serious balance of payment crisis in the history of the region".[33]

HIV TARGETS THE MOST VULNERABLE

It is clear that AIDS epidemics have the potential to derail development in the most seriously-affected Third World communities, and to slow progress in many others. And in the United States at least, though not apparently in Europe, AIDS is especially hitting ethnic minorities, which are already disproportionately affected by multiple forms of deprivation.

These communities are doubly vulnerable. First, as a result of many social, economic, health and behavioural factors, their members may possibly be more susceptible to infection by HIV and, once infected, more vulnerable to a progression to AIDS. The accumulating, but as yet incomplete, evidence which relates HIV transmission patterns to these factors is discussed in Chapters Three and Six.

The second aspect of vulnerability is the individual or community's reduced capacity to defend itself against AIDS. Both in the Third World and in minority communities in the North, multiple disadvantages — illiteracy, lack of material and human resources, insufficient transport and communications networks, economic collapse, social breakdown due to war or migration, a burden of racial or other discrimination leading to low self-esteem and self-destructive behaviour patterns — all combine to limit the community's capacity to fight the epidemic.

The predominantly white northern homosexual communities, first hit by AIDS and therefore most experienced in organising to combat it, show some interesting parallels with the obstacles to AIDS education among Third World and northern minority groups. Homosexual men's groups in the United States and Europe went through four common stages in AIDS awareness: first, denial of the problem; second, recognition of the problem; third, mobilisation of resources for community education; and fourth, behaviour change leading to reduced transmission of the virus.

As a number of books and articles written by homosexual men testify, the move from denial to recognition was achieved only with difficulty.

THE DANGERS OF DENIAL

Randy Shilts, an author long familiar with both AIDS and the homosexual lifestyle, has documented the "denial factor" in San Francisco and New York in the early years of the epidemic.[34] While not everyone agrees with his analysis, his book gives a useful insight into the attitudes of the period. Some homosexual men and some of their organisations feared that an admission that AIDS existed and was attacking their communities would endanger their status and lifestyle. To admit openly that AIDS was attacking their communities would, they believed, invite repression from homophobic groups, endanger hard-won victories against discrimination, and force homosexual men back on the defensive.

A prominent New York homosexual author, Larry Kramer, has written a successful play dramatising this period of denial in the homosexual community. [35] The play shows how an initially small group of homosexual activists in New York City rejected the denial syndrome and in 1982 created Gay Mens' Health Crisis, a community-based group which grew to become one of the most effective AIDS organisations in the United States. Even in 1983, after AIDS had struck more than 1,000 people in the United States, most of them homosexual, national homosexual lobbying organisations were failing to take a lead in seeking funds and civil rights protection against AIDS.

But once past the stage of denial, homosexual groups in the United States and Europe had economic and other advantages which allowed them to organise and adapt quickly. Experience shows that Third World and ethnic minority communities are no less likely to deny at first that AIDS is a serious problem. But, once past this stage, their potential for action is often severely limited.

The next chapter describes the impact of AIDS on various communities: first, on three US ethnic minority groups, and then on four groups in the Caribbean, Africa and Asia.

CHAPTER THREE

PORTRAITS OF VULNERABILITY

New York City health authorities estimate that one in 15 of the population may have already been infected with the HIV virus. From 1979 to February 1988, more than 13,000 cases of AIDS had been reported in the city. But these statistics hide the way in which the virus has recently been selecting its victims, since over half of the city's reported cases of AIDS are among minorities: black, hispanic or Asian.

Of New York women with AIDS, 84% are from minority groups; the disease is the major cause of death among women aged 25-34. Epidemiologists predict that by 1991 AIDS in New York City will be the largest killer of women in their childbearing years. To date, 92% of the over 250 children in New York who have developed AIDS have been born to minority mothers.

Though blacks and hispanics together comprise 45% of New York City's population, they account for 56% of the AIDS cases; countrywide they comprise 19% of the population, but 39% of cases. [1]

Most minority men who contract the virus do so as a result of homosexual encounters or intravenous drug use; the women are usually infected through injecting drugs or through heterosexual contact with an infected man.

As well as being more liable to be infected with the virus, black or hispanic people may die sooner from AIDS. While the average lifespan of a US white person after diagnosis is two years, the average minority person survives only 19 weeks. Comparatively fewer doctors work in minority communities, and their patients are socially and financially less likely to seek early treatment. Minority patients with AIDS are likely to be less healthy than their white counterparts before they contract the virus, a fact relating to their lower social and economic status. By the time they present themselves for treatment their symptoms may already be far advanced.

HEROIN AND A HARLEM FAMILY: LISA'S STORY

The impact of AIDS on minority groups has been felt heavily in the city's downtown core. Manhattan borough president David N. Dinkins has for some time been drawing attention to the toll which AIDS is taking among blacks and hispanics. "Six years into this epidemic, there are few residents of the borough I represent who can say they don't know, or don't know of, someone who has died [of AIDS]. As with most crises, AIDS does not exist apart from other chronic problems we face in our cities. The connections among AIDS and poverty, drug abuse, limited access to health care, the housing shortage, discrimination, illiteracy and other barriers to AIDS prevention and treatment must be acknowledged and explored. AIDS is not only the product of certain risk activities, but also of social and economic conditions which place entire communities of New York City at greater risk than others."[2]

Lisa (not her real name) is a young black woman from New York City. She is a heroin addict; she has AIDS; and she has three children. Her husband and her baby son have both died of AIDS; her daughter is HIV-positive. Lisa has survived three years since being diagnosed with AIDS, and in August 1987 she wrote her story for Panos in the hope that others might learn from it.

"I am 32 years old, the third of 14 children. We were poor and lived in Harlem. Most of my childhood was spent in foster homes or shelters, because my stepfather abused me. After one attack I had to go to the hospital and he spent two years in jail. I dropped out of school in the tenth grade. I got involved with a drug dealer and in no time I had the habit [injecting heroin]. I was still a kid, but I felt much older.

"When I got pregnant at 15 I thought at last I'm going to have someone I can really love and everything will be all right. How wrong I was! I couldn't care for her and I got so depressed I went back to drugs and gave my daughter to my mother to raise. She's 14 now and has already had an abortion.

"My next child, a boy, was born addicted to heroin. I can't forgive myself for getting high all the time I was carrying him. While his father was in jail I tried to be a good mother. I moved from Harlem to Brooklyn to get away from people who only knew me as a drug user. For two years I did fine, but I got lonely and the only thing that ever made me feel good was drugs. So I started again. Before long I was on the fast road, getting high every day. It's funny how many people want to be your friend when they know you are weak.

"In 1984 my son was in and out of the hospital and the doctors couldn't tell me what was wrong. Then his father came home from jail. We noticed how sick and small he was; like our son, he was so weak his legs could hardly carry him. In 1985 the doctor at Harlem Hospital told us his father had AIDS from shooting drugs. I knew in my heart that my little boy also had this sickness, but I didn't want to believe it because I didn't know children could get AIDS. When the doctor confirmed it I felt so helpless.

"I had been in and out of the hospital too, so I decided to be tested. The day the doctor told me I had AIDS I wanted to give up, but how could I take the easy way out when my son was still hanging on like a little trooper? So now all three of us were sick together, but my son's father mostly stayed in the hospital. Eventually AIDS went to his brain, killing him at 33.

"Soon my son got so weak I asked God to take away his pain. The day he died he wanted everyone near him. He started to choke and his eyes rolled back. We took him to hospital, but they couldn't save him. I can't explain my feelings: I was glad there was no more pain for him, but I still wanted him with me. I would do anything if I could change things. It hurt so much seeing his little body in that all-white casket and leaving the cemetery without him.

"I'm still holding on because I now have a little girl who is four years old. With luck and the help of God she will be all right."

In March 1988 Panos learned that Lisa's situation had worsened. Her daughter, now five, had tested HIV-positive and was now showing AIDS-related symptoms. Lisa made a suicide attempt. While she was in hospital her stepbrother died of syphilis and AIDS in a ward one floor below. Although Lisa initially moved back with her mother, she was forced to leave after her stepfather once again attempted to rape her. She is now living with a half-brother, and she is so despondent she is again injecting drugs.

FARM-WORKERS IN BELLE GLADE, FLORIDA

Belle Glade is only 40 miles away from West Palm Beach, one of America's lushest and most affluent communities.

Flat and baking fields of sugarcane surround the town, where upwards of 20,000 people live in conditions as remote from Palm Beach as it is possible to get. They include black migrant farm workers whose material level of existence is straight out of a textbook on extremes of poverty.

All the contagious diseases of overcrowding and poor sanitation have been documented in Belle Glade's black ghetto, where the population, with a high percentage of single men, is squashed into a few acres of shacks and boardinghouses. Mean housing once built for seasonal workers have become permanent homes which provide all the requisites of squalor: communal toilets, outdoor sinks, leaking sewers, inadequate garbage disposal.

"Toilet facilities are so disgusting in many of these buildings that if they were located in the county jail I could go to federal court and get an order to either clean them up or shut them down ," says K. Stuart Goldberg, director of the Florida Rural Legal Services Office, a group which provides the poor with legal assistance.[3] Even so, the shacks are better than living as some families do, in an abandoned car or bus.

Some 5,000 farm workers live year-round in these conditions, their numbers swelled during the cane harvest by thousands more migrant workers — West Indians, Haitians, Cubans and Mexicans — who live in sugar mill compounds on the edge of town. Supplying vegetables to the rest of North America and to Europe, the region also hosts thousands of illegal Mexican workers who harvest the salads now enjoyed now in those places throughout the winter.

Belle Glade achieved national prominence in 1983 when AIDS cases were first diagnosed there. By 1985 state health officials believed that the per capita rate at which AIDS cases were appearing might be the highest in the world. Several of the first cases appeared in Haitians, but soon the virus was gaining access to all of Belle Glade's people through the twin routes of intravenous drug addiction and sexual contact.

Both men and women are infected, with the seasonal to-and-froing of labourers a near-guarantee that the virus is being carried out of Belle Glade and back to the workers' home communities abroad.

GERALDO: A SALVADOREAN ILLEGAL IN THE UNITED STATES

Between three and six million people currently live illegally in the United States. They share an uncertain status and future. Objects of discrimination and exploitation, their often tenuous hold on the mainstream of American life renders many of them vulnerable to AIDS.

Most of the immigrants from Central America are young men, aged 15-40, fleeing army service and looking for work in "El Norte". Many have only a primary school education — and no legal papers. Distinct streams of migration have developed, with Guatemalans and urban Salvadoreans heading for Los Angeles, San Francisco and Texas; rural Salvadoreans to Washington DC and Long Island, New York; Nicaraguans to Miami; and Hondurans to New Orleans.

Geraldo (not his real name) is a homosexual Salvadorean draughtsman who lives in Washington DC. An illegal immigrant, he had never heard of AIDS until he was diagnosed as having it himself. He now spends much of his time educating Salvadoreans and other immigrants in the United States about the dangers of AIDS. His story here is translated from Spanish, in an interview in October 1987 with Patricia Ardila, a Colombian journalist currently based in Washington DC.

"I left San Salvador in 1981 and came to Washington DC where an uncle of mine has lived for the last 20 years. My sister, who is a social worker, came here just before me."

"Why did you leave El Salvador?"

"Because I lost my job as a draughtsman. At that time I was working for a construction company in San Salvador. But the firm had to close down due to the economic crisis the country has been experiencing since the beginning of the civil war. And then I could not get another job.

"Another reason was the war itself. In 1981 there were daily confrontations in the streets of San Salvador between the army and the guerrilla forces. Everybody felt threatened by the death squads, whether you were a militant or not. At the the beginning of 1981 I learned of three homosexuals who were arrested by the security forces without any reason, and then killed after being sexually abused by those guys. Once I realised that the situation was becoming extremely difficult down there I decided to leave."

"What kind of jobs have you had since your arrival?"

"I have been really lucky because since the very beginning I have been able to hold on to jobs: one during the day in an hispanic grocery store, and another at night in a restaurant. So I have had enough money to pay the rent, utilities, and food. But then I got this disease."

"When did you get AIDS and how do you think you got it?"

"I had never heard of AIDS before I was diagnosed with it. In August 1986 I had fever for three consecutive weeks. I also lost my appetite and was losing weight — too much weight. First I thought I had syphilis again (I had it in 1985), so I went to the "Clinica del Pueblo" (a medical centre for Salvadoreans) to see the doctor. I also had a blood test but they told me that I did not have any venereal disease. But the fever continued and I felt extremely weak. I couldn't go to work anymore.

"Then my sister suggested to me that perhaps I had contracted AIDS. She didn't know then that I was a homosexual, but when she told me about high risk groups and so on, I told her I was gay. She was very nice to me and gave me some articles on AIDS. Before that, I never heard a word about it.

"I went to the Whitman Walker Clinic (for homosexuals), but they also told me that I didn't have any infection. I now know that the problem was that I went on Saturday, but they only do the blood tests for AIDS on Wednesdays. So I only had a routine blood test and the virus of course did not show up. At the end of September I went to the George Washington Hospital, and for three days the doctors performed all sort of exams on me. I was diagnosed as having AIDS as well as pneumonia carinii." [Pneumocystis carinii is a type of pneumonia frequently found in AIDS patients.]

"Geraldo, how is it possible that you never heard of AIDS before your sister mentioned it to you? Since 1983 all the newspapers, magazines and TV programmes have been dealing with AIDS continuously."

"Well, the problem is I had two jobs, so I did not have time to read newspapers or watch television. I usually got home at one or two in the morning, and I just went to bed. And when I went to the gay bars looking for company, I went right to the point in that situation you don't talk too much! Having sex with these men from the bars was actually the main problem because I am sure I got the disease from somebody I met in one of those places. I'll bet he did not know about AIDS either. So what happened was that people were spreading the virus for a long time without being aware that they had it."

"What happened after you left the hospital? Did the doctors give you any treatment?"

"When I was there the doctors gave me some medicine but I do not know what it was. Then I went home and for two months I had to stay in bed because I felt really weak. Sometimes I couldn't even breathe. Then in January of this year my sister learned that doctors at the George Washington Hospital were looking for volunteers to be treated experimentally with a new drug called AZT. So I sent my application with all the appropriate information about my condition. I was selected to be treated with the drug."

"Has AZT helped you to feel better?"

"Yes. It has improved my condition somewhat, although sometimes it makes me feel lazy. It is not that I really am lazy, but I don't feel like doing anything but resting. Now I can only work for a few hours a day. I work for a programme which provides sexual education for hispanics here in Washington. My job consists of talking to small groups of people about AIDS and other venereal diseases so they can avoid them. The programme has an AIDS hot-line, and I am one of those responsible for answering people's questions on the disease."

"How did you learn about the programme?"

"I didn't learn about it — they learned about me! This is because I decided to give interviews to some hispanic newspapers and to the hispanic television channel here in Washington about my case. Even though nobody likes to raise his hand and say 'Hey! I have AIDS', I decided to tell my story so people will become aware of the problem and help to stop spreading the virus. My sister and my compañero, the man with whom I share my life, told me that I could help others. That is why I am talking about AIDS. It's no joke."

"Who is paying for your treatment? I understood that it is really expensive."

"Yes it is, and soon that will be a problem. At the beginning I was not paying anything since I was an experiment volunteer. Now the drug has been approved and commercialised so I will have to pay for it. I still have a small supply, but once it is finished I'll be in trouble because I have been told that it will cost between $7,000 and $8,000 a year to get what I need. I have to take a pill every four hours."

"What are you going to do then?"

"I have decided to apply for the amnesty the government is offering for those of us illegals who came here before January 1982. Once I become legal, I can apply for government-funded medicare to get AZT. Right now I am in the process of filling out my application form since I have all the documents and certificates that the immigration authorities are requesting."

"Geraldo, you know that the INS (Immigration and Naturalization Service) is requesting all applicants for amnesty to be tested for AIDS?"

"Yes, I have heard about it, but that will not happen yet. According to the new immigration law, people who may be eligible for amnesty will be given a temporary work permit if they fulfil all the requirements. That work permit is good for 18 months after which you have to apply for permanent residence. It is then when people will be tested for AIDS."

"What will you do if , after the 18 months are over and you have to apply for permanent residence, the immigration authorities ask you to be tested for AIDS?"

"Who knows? I have been told that AZT helps to hide the virus when you are tested. Perhaps it will not show up. So maybe I will test negative." [Editor's note: Geraldo's information on this point is incorrect]. "I try not to think too much about it. The only thing I can tell you is that at least here I will have access to the medicine I need. I do not even think about going back to El Salvador, although my parents have told me to do so, so they can take care of me. Of course they know I am very ill, but they do not know what my illness is all about.

"But what am I going to do back home if I cannot get AZT? And the government here in the United States — how can it deny people with AIDS the opportunity to come here for treatment, if the medicine is not available anywhere else? I hope the authorities will change their minds about sending people back or not allowing people with AIDS to come here for medical treatment."

Geraldo's situation is likely to be repeated, no one knows yet how many times over, among several million illegals in the United States who are expected to apply for amnesty. Those who can prove they have resided continuously in the United States since January 1982 will be allowed to legalise their status and remain. The rest will be forced to return to their countries of origin. Those applying to stay will be subject to mandatory blood tests for the AIDS virus; those found to be HIV-positive will be deported.

It is not known how many of the illegal residents in the United States are presently carriers of the virus, but Geraldo's story shows that some of them are. Those who are infected, and who return to their own countries, will either knowingly or unknowingly take the virus back with them, to add to the already growing epidemic of HIV infection south of the US border.

CITÉ SOLEIL, HAITI

In cities like London and Geneva, governments alerted the populace to the threat of AIDS by putting a booklet through the mailbox of each house. In the slum of Cité Soleil, part of the Haitian capital of Port au Prince, even housing itself is hard to come by. A ramshackle urban shantytown, its cheapest tin-and-cardboard shelters can be beyond the means of the average family, so sleeping is done in shifts.

Haiti has reported 1,155 cases of AIDS, with an unofficial total surpassing 1,500. With one of the world's higher per capita AIDS case rates, Haiti has one of the lowest per capita incomes and one of the most degraded environments in the developing world.

In Port au Prince, one of every 10 people could, it is thought, already be infected by the virus. Perhaps half of the capital's prostitutes are carriers, and medical experts fear that the virus is being spread to rural areas, where three quarters of the population lives. In the cities there is one doctor for every 5,000 people; in the countryside there is one for 40,000 or more. Viral and parasitic infections are common, and in the absence of physicians people turn to untrained practitioners called "piqûristes", known for their ready hand with a syringe — usually an unsterilised one.

Of Haiti's first AIDS cases, appearing in 1978-9, 65% were in men who had slept with North American homosexuals. These cases were not investigated until 1982. Only 12% of cases were in women. But by 1986 homosexuals or bisexuals accounted for only 7% of male Haitian AIDS cases, and 40% of the total cases were women. Together with the absence of the AIDS virus from blood samples drawn in Haiti in 1977-79, epidemiological considerations suggest that the virus may have been introduced to Haiti from the United States, and not the other way round.[4]

PROSTITUTION AS A RISK ACTIVITY

Olongapo in the Philippines is home to the largest US naval base outside the mainland United States. Prostitution is illegal, so officially there are no prostitutes. But there are 5,000-6,000 registered "hospitality women" in Olangapo town, and an additional 10,000 or more working in the surrounding region. Hospitality women are typically young women from rural areas who seek employment in an industry for which their lack of education prepares them. They see work in the sex trade as a temporary expedient on the way to the longer term goal of marriage and a family. They may average three or four partners a week.[5]

Before the location of the naval base there, prostitution was unthought of as a means of livelihood. But with the Vietnam War the base became the busiest port in the Western Pacific, drawing young women from the country's poorest provinces. Hospitality girls work seven days a week, but they do not prosper. Under conditions little different from slavery, their on or off duty movements are controlled by the bar owners who pay them, their distress submerged in drugs.

Blood tests show that by 1987 43 hospitality women in Olangapo had contracted the AIDS virus. Filipino health authorities have recognised that, if they are to prevent a full-scale AIDS epidemic in the country, they will not only have to screen hospitality women and prevent those infected with HIV from working, but to assist the women in finding economic self- sufficiency outside prostitution. Six of the 43 positive women have become pregnant despite warnings from the health authorities that their infants could be born carrying the virus. Three of the women have delivered, and while doctors want to monitor the infants' progress, some of the women have failed to return for check-ups despite a monetary incentive.[6]

Economics appear to have a lot to do with the degree of risk — from HIV and other sexually transmitted infections — which prostitutes face, especially in the fastest growing Third World cities where at present men tend to outnumber women and well-paid jobs for women are scarce. In Nairobi, Kenya, during 1986 women belonging to a group of lower socio-economic group prostitutes were found to average more than 900 sexual encounters per year, for which they earned 50 US cents per encounter: a yearly income of less than $500. On average the women had been working in this manner for six years. More than half the women reacted positively to a test for syphilis, 45% had gonorrhoea, and 42% had genital ulcers.[7]

Most of the women had been drawn to the bustle and relative prosperity of Nairobi from towns and villages, some from neighbouring countries like Tanzania and Uganda. Typically they have only primary school education and are ill-equipped to compete on the job market. So instead of finding the job, the good time, or the husband of their dreams, most of these women found HIV. Between 1983 and 1986, more than half of them contracted the AIDS virus, a proportion rising to 88% by the end of 1987.[8]

When we think of prostitutes, we tend to think of women or girls, but HIV is revealing how inaccurate this image is. In the Thai capital of Bangkok, health centres have been testing prostitutes for exposure to the AIDS virus. The prostitutes work in Thailand's thriving sex industry, which caters to tourists flush with hard currency from North America, Europe, Australia and Japan. Of the female prostitutes tested in 1987, only 0.05% were HIV seropositive. But among male prostitutes, usually in their teens and early twenties, 2.6% tested positive.[9]

Only some of the male sex workers will class themselves as homosexual, for many of them have girlfriends and will eventually marry. They are simply earning a living by one of the few means available to them in an economy dominated by tourism and the need for foreign exchange. They resemble the Haitian male prostitutes who, early in that country's AIDS epidemic, unknowingly passed the virus from their tourist customers to their wives and girlfriends.

BLACK SOUTH AFRICANS

For the 20 million black people in South Africa's "homelands", life is often nasty, brutish and short. For every wage earner who manages to gain employment in a city outside the homeland, many more depend on the salary he or she sends home. Families are split between homeland and township, with neither part having enough to wear, shelter under or eat. Over half of black children under the age of five are stunted through malnutrition. Among adults, it is common to find tuberculosis, viral and parasitic infections, sexually transmitted diseases, and mental illnesses such as depression leading to suicide.

Of the 76 AIDS cases in South African nationals reported by January 1988, over 85% have been in white homosexual men. In 1986 blood test surveys on 30,000 black migrant mine workers showed that 3.8% of those from Malawi were seropositive, as were 0.3% of those from Botswana.[10] By the end of 1986, the South African Chamber of Mines reported that 130 miners had been found to be infected with the AIDS virus, [11] the number rising to over 1,000 by September 1987.[12] The virus has also been found to be present among black women who have had sexual relations with the mineworkers, who live in barracks away from their families for most of the year.

In early 1987 the Kenyan Red Cross (left) and the Ugandan Government (right) published leaflets on AIDS and how to avoid it.

Mine companies have provided workers with some information about AIDS, but the government's policy on AIDS control is to keep infected workers out by testing them for the virus in their countries of origin. Workers who test positive in South Africa are expelled. Those who live in neighbouring states and apply to work in South Africa are tested in their own countries and refused entry if found to be seropositive.

In South Africa, the AIDS virus has already found a situation which provides it with maximum opportunity: an uprooted, suppressed, materially deprived black population in which infectious disease is already epidemic and among whom distrust of the white authorities is ingrained from birth. Illiteracy promoted by restricted education, and the suspicion with which the use of condoms is greeted (promoted as part of birth control campaigns, they are regarded by blacks as a tool of white genocidal aspiration) will ensure the minimal impact of any AIDS information effort led by white officialdom.

AN EAST AFRICAN TRUCKER

After two decades of civil strife, and with more than half a million deaths, social and economic life in Uganda has been subject to sustained stress. In better times, the Ugandan shilling and the Kenyan shilling were worth the same; now, Uganda's currency is worth 300 times less. By the mid-1970s smuggling and barter along the Tanzanian border took place in a "live for today" atmosphere, which fostered casual sexual relationships.

Anxiety, depression and shock accompanied epidemics of measles, malaria, tuberculosis and sexually transmitted diseases. Public services crumbled, and health spending fell to near zero. Enter the AIDS virus, probably during the late 1970s, with Uganda's first case diagnosed in the village of Kansensero in 1982.

By 1986, blood surveys were revealing that, among sexually active adults attending outpatient clinics in southwest Uganda, over 30% were carriers of the virus. In Kampala, home to half a million people, about 10% of adult blood donors and 13% of pregnant women tested HIV-seropositive, and in small surveys in Gulu, a town about 150 miles north of Kampala, bloodtests on women attending prenatal clinics showed similar results.

By March 1988, Uganda had reported 2,369 cases of AIDS and Tanzania 1,608. Both governments have recognised the seriousness of the AIDS epidemic, devised national strategies for combating the disease and secured pledges of assistance from foreign donors. Damaged transport and communications handicap Uganda's efforts to mobilise on the health front, and in many areas there are persistent shortages of essential but relatively simple items, such as bleach for disinfecting hospital equipment, rubber gloves and even paper for posters.

Sexually transmitted diseases in East Africa, as in many other developing countries, are almost an "occupational hazard" among certain groups — bar girls and prostitutes, taxi and truck drivers, musicians, salesmen, soldiers and sailors: urban dwellers whose profession or financial status leads them to travel or work away from a traditional family grouping.

Peter, a 42 year old Kenyan (his real name is not used, at his request), has for the past 11 years been a long-haul truck driver. A pleasant, sturdy man with an aura of competence, he has woven about himself an "extended" family of a non-traditional variety, made up of the many friends he makes en route. "It's good to have friends", he says. "Wherever I go I have someone to talk to, to eat and drink with, so I'm never lonely". Peter's routine requires driving for periods of several weeks at a time between Sudan, Ethiopia, Uganda, Zaire, Tanzania, Zambia and Botswana — countries separated by distances·

31

equal to half the length of the African continent, and through some of the worst AIDS-affected countries in the world.

Peter's "real" family, a wife and seven children live in Nairobi, where he visits them for a few days about once a month. But, he says, "the people I meet on the road, in the restaurants and bars and hostels, they are also like family to me. I meet the same people often, and there are quite a few women who are my girlfriends. They have other boyfriends too, but I bring them presents and they are always happy to see me." Does he like his job? "Yes, I like it a lot. I can move around, see new things, and the pay is good so I can afford the childrens' schooling — and that makes my wife happy."[13]

Peter is not, of course, typical of East Africans in the large number of girlfriends he has, spread through several countries. But just as a minority of sexually-active and well-travelled homosexual men in the United States played a large role in the initial spread of AIDS there, Peter is an example of those individuals in the Third World whose lifestyle makes them both vulnerable to AIDS, and unfortunately likely to spread it.

CHAPTER FOUR

ORIGINS OF AIDS, ORIGINS OF BLAME

"What is more important than knowing where this disease came from is where it is going." — President Kenneth Kaunda of Zambia, October 1987.

When a new and deadly disease appears, it is natural to want to know where it has come from. So far, we do *not* know the origins of the HIV virus which causes AIDS.

Much scientific effort (and far more wholly non-scientific speculation) has been devoted to this question. Unfortunately, the debate about the origins of AIDS has become hopelessly mixed with questions of who — which country, which race, is to *blame* for starting the epidemic. We shall return to the debate about blame later in this book: Chapters Four and Five are devoted mainly to the scientific evidence.

Since we know how HIV is transmitted (mother-to-foetus, infected blood, and sex), it is usually possible to work out how each AIDS patient became infected — or it would be, if everyone was willing to be wholly frank about their past sexual encounters, which few people are.

EARLY CASES: THE US, AFRICA, EUROPE, HAITI

In theory it ought to be possible to find out when and where the first case of AIDS occurred. In practice, this is not so easy. The medical condition which was later to be called AIDS began to be noticed in the late 1970s and early 1980s in several widely separated locations, including Belgium, France, Haiti, the United States, Zaire and Zambia.

As they learnt to diagnose AIDS, and in an effort to better understand just what they were up against, medical investigators in the United States and elsewhere began to look backwards in time, seeking the "first case" of the new disease. Step by step, this quest has led as far back as 1959, where the trail, for the present at least, runs cold.

The first medical reports of the syndrome soon to be named AIDS were published in the United States in June 1981.[1] For two years preceding these reports, a small but growing number of homosexual men and their physicians in New York City, Los Angeles and San Francisco were noticing rare or unusual disease symptoms — *pneumocystis* pneumonia, Kaposi's sarcoma in young men and a host of infections not found in otherwise healthy people. These ailments seemed to be related to inexplicable deterioration in the men's immune systems.[2]

Powerless to help these patients, or even to explain what had gone wrong with their bodies' defences, the doctors began to suspect the existence of a new, sexually transmitted infection. Doctors at the US Centers for Disease Control (CDC) in Atlanta, Georgia, also began to suspect that blood transmission could also be a factor: similar symptoms were being recorded among intravenous drug users. By the end of 1981, records would later show that in the United States the disease had claimed the lives of 248 people.

By the end of 1981, doctors in the Zairean capital of Kinshasa had also begun to document dozens of cases where their patients' multiple infections seemed to relate to a collapse of the body's immune function.[3] And in Zambia the appearance of a new and more aggressive form of Kaposi's sarcoma, linked with immune deficiencies, prompted a physician working there to observe the similarity between the symptoms of her Zambian patients and those which had broken out among American homosexuals.[4]

As the medical profession started to track backwards through the 1970s, it became clear that some of the earliest known cases of AIDS had been seen by Belgian doctors in Africans. The first seems to have been a 34 year old Zairean airline secretary, who flew to Belgium with her child late in 1977, to find out the reason for their persistent respiratory and intestinal infections.[5]

Late 1980 and early 1981 saw doctors at a Parisian clinic baffled by a case of *pneumocystis* pneumonia in a Portuguese man recently arrived from Angola, in a Zairean woman, and in a French woman who had recently lived in Zaire.[6] Of the first 200 patients affected by the new disease in Europe, 42 were African.[7]

In Haiti the tell-tale combination of Kaposi's sarcoma and uncontrollable opportunistic infections seems, in retrospect, first to have appeared in 1978-9,[8] coinciding with the earliest cases of Kaposi's sarcoma in homosexual men in the United States, and with the arrival of the first African patients with the new disease in Europe. Haitian refugees with immunodeficiency disease were seen in increasing numbers in New York City and Miami during 1980/81. By mid-1982 the CDC had documented 34 such cases.[9] By October 1982 researchers in Haiti had diagnosed 61 cases.

The roughly simultaneous appearance of AIDS in the United States,

Europe, Africa and Haiti prompted the question: had AIDS been around for some time, unnoticed because the characteristic collection of opportunistic infections so indicative of underlying immune impairment had not been recognised?

After combing through medical histories of past patients, investigators found a small number of probable cases of AIDS going back nearly 30 years on three continents. Working back in time they found AIDS-like symptoms in patients as early as 1959:

** **1979**: a 44 year old homosexual man died with Kaposi's sarcoma in New York City;[10]

** **1977**: a 27 year old Rwandan mother developed the novel immunodeficiency symptoms;[11]

** **1977**: the 34 year old Zairean woman mentioned above who sought treatment in Belgium; she died in Kinshasa in 1978;[12]

** **1977**: a 47 year old Danish surgeon who had worked in rural Zaire died in Denmark;[13]

** **1975**: a previously healthy seven-month old black infant had pneumocystis in New York City;[14]

** **1969**: a 15 year old black US boy died with Kaposi's sarcoma and opportunistic infections in St Louis;[15]

** **1959**: a British sailor with Kaposi's sarcoma and pneumocystis died in Manchester;[16]

** **1959**: a 45 year old US man born in Haiti died;[17]

In a few of these cases the retrospective diagnoses of AIDS are now supported by positive blood tests for HIV. Most, however, have been identified as possible early cases of AIDS on the basis of symptoms alone. The search goes on, and it is possible that eventually earlier possible cases will be found somewhere.

The further back in time such medical detective work extends, however, the more uncertain the retrospective diagnoses tend to become. People do not die of AIDS itself, for AIDS is not really a disease but a syndrome of opportunistic infections which strike when immune functioning has been impaired by HIV. To determine retrospectively whether the infections that killed them were actually part of the syndrome is guesswork at best.

TESTING OLD BLOOD

If people had been dying since 1959 from what now appears to have been AIDS, they must have become infected by the HIV virus some years before that. In the mid-1980s medical researchers started to test old samples of blood which had originally been drawn for other purposes, and then stored for decades in laboratory freezers.

At this time — the mid-eighties — it was widely assumed by the medical profession that AIDS had originated in Africa, partly because the early European cases had African links, and partly because it was thought unlikely that such an unusual disease could have gone unnoticed for long in the United States. Therefore much of this early blood research — the results of which were to prove highly controversial — was directed at Africa.

The first batches of stored African blood samples were tested by US scientists using a type of test much less reliable than many of those available today.[18] Their results, which have since been discredited, claimed to show the presence of HIV antibodies in over 50% of stored blood samples which had been drawn in Kenya and Uganda in the 1960s and 70s. Other researchers who lived and worked in Africa carried out tests on stored blood samples and found no evidence of such early infection by HIV. None of the samples drawn from elderly people during these decades in Uganda's West Nile district were seropositive, for example.[19]

Because the first erroneous results implied that AIDS was endemic in central Africa, they received widespread attention in the media. Less well reported were large blood surveys carried out around the same time which showed much lower levels of infection. Using a different type of test than that employed by the US researchers whose results were mistaken, another group found that of 1,000 blood samples drawn in Kinshasa in 1970, only 2% were seropositive. This finding was announced at the first international conference on AIDS in Brussels in June 1985 but failed to attract the same extensive media interest.[20]

Similar research on stored blood samples drawn from North Americans and Europeans in the 1960s and 1970s could have been performed, since samples were available for this purpose. However, it seems that such testing was not carried out.*

TESTING BLOOD IN THE TROPICS

The early false positive results contributed to many confusions and misunderstandings about the history of HIV and AIDS. While more improved tests are now available which help to minimise false positive results, it remains the case that some types of tests are more appropriate than others for use in the tropics, where hot climates make

*The earliest available blood survey data from tests carried out on stored blood in the United States is from samples taken from homosexual men in San Francisco in 1978, 4% proving seropositive.[21]

unintentional bacterial contamination of blood samples more likely. Such samples are prone to give false results since they become "sticky", as does stored blood which has been repeatedly frozen and thawed. Moreover, in rural tropical areas where people commonly suffer multiple parasitic infections, such as malaria, schistosomiasis, tuberculosis or various worm infestations, problems of interpretation can make the accurate reading of HIV antibody tests very difficult. Because the immune systems of such multiply-infected people are in a chronically activated state, HIV antibody tests can be confounded by excessive antibody "noise".

The problem of ensuring accurate readings when testing "sticky" or "noisy" blood samples has been approached in different ways. A US approach is to subject samples which appear on the first test to contain HIV antibodies to a second, confirmatory test, usually one known as the Western Blot. Only samples which are also shown to contain HIV antibodies by Western Blot are considered to be truly positive. The second approach is put forward mainly by British researchers. Their quarrel with the US method is that it employs two tests which, though, better than one, are too similar to rule out false positive results on tricky blood samples, particularly in the tropics. The British employ not only two tests, but two types of test, which are very different from one another, so that any weakness in the first is compensated by the second.[22]

Testing blood for antibodies to the AIDS virus is a complicated business and like any form of screening or diagnostic test, the results are not infallible. Nevertheless, during the three years in which HIV antibody detection tests have been in use, great improvements in their sensitivity and specificity have been made and this is as true in Africa as elsewhere. Unfortunately, accurate results today cannot erase the legacy of early inaccurate results which led to the labelling of Africa as the "AIDS continent". Says Dr Richard Tedder, who participated in the development of a respected British test: "Bad results in the early days of testing muddied the waters and this is what many people tend to remember. They level the accusation that "you scientists got it wrong once, why should we believe your results are any better now?" Explaining that there are different types of tests and that some are better than others, is not always convincing for people whose suspicions have been aroused. It's understandable but unfortunate that some Africans tend to take the view that any and all serological results are questionable."[23]

BACK-TRACKING THE AIDS VIRUS

In the United States the presence of antibodies to HIV was recently detected in the stored blood and tissues of the New Orleans teenager mentioned above who died in 1969. These samples had been kept because the physicians who treated him say they were so puzzled by his symptoms that they stored specimens for future research which might help to explain his illness,[24] To date the earliest known blood sample registering seropositive by means of several different antibody tests was drawn in Kinshasa, Zaire, in 1959.[25]

The history of AIDS has also been investigated in a less scientific way, by going back to the earliest North American cases, and asking friends of AIDS patients about their sex lives, in an attempt to identify the original "Patient Zero". One unproved suggestion is that US cases all go back to a homosexual Air Canada steward who infected a large number of people across North America. No-one knows where this man caught the disease or if this suggestion is true.[26] There is little scientific evidence for this back- tracking, since the key witnesses are now dead. Even if true, it does not help answer the question of how the AIDS virus came to exist in the first place.

Neither medical nor journalistic enquiry has managed to trace HIV infection further back than 1959, when the HIV trail as it has so far been traced in Africa and the United States peters out. What could have accounted for the sudden appearance of this seemingly new and deadly virus?

HIV: HOW THE VIRUS SURVIVES

The first suspected cases of AIDS, and of HIV infection, at present do not go back before 1959. So the HIV virus which causes AIDS could have been around at least since the mid-1950s. Where and how did it emerge?

At the end of World War II, only a handful of human viruses were known. Hundreds more have been discovered since, partly as a result of advanced techniques for culturing them in the laboratory. Viruses are parasites which infect almost every form of life, from single-celled bacteria up to humans.

In evolutionary terms, host and virus populations engage in skirmishes, which most often result in the elimination of the viral infection by the host's immune system. Influenza, measles and polio are examples of viral disease which, more often than not, our bodies combat successfully, rendering us immune to subsequent infection by the same virus. These diseases have short incubation periods of days or weeks between infection and the appearance of symptoms, and the symptoms themselves are generally short-lived. In order to maintain its existence within the host community, the virus must pass from infected to uninfected individuals within this short period, or risk being eliminated as an increasing number of hosts develop protective immunity. The virus in this case requires a very large host population

— in the case of measles in excess of 100,000 individuals — in order to survive.

In certain other types of illness, however, the virus employs a different survival strategy. After infecting the host and triggering an initial acute bout of symptoms, viruses such as those of the herpes family stop producing any obvious sickness and become latent, living unnoticed in the host's cells for months or years until conditions are right for the triggering off of another acute outburst of symptoms. **Latent viruses can survive in small host populations by making their hosts periodically infective during the acute phases of the illness.**

A third viral survival strategy features aspects of the above two approaches. Combining infectivity which lasts for much of the duration of the illness (as with measles), with persistence in the host's body long after the first symptoms appear (as with herpes), viruses like those causing Hepatitis B and AIDS seem to cause lifelong infections, during which time the host is capable of transmitting the virus to others.

Persistent viral infections can be sustained over long periods of time in small host communities. They can, in theory at least, be spread to a new and uninfected host population by a single carrier. When the disease they cause breaks out, with deceptive suddenness, months or years later, it may well be impossible to trace how or when the infection was first introduced. This persistence explains why the exact event which marks the beginnings of an AIDS epidemic in a given community can so rarely be identified, but it does not explain where the AIDS virus came from in the first place.

REPORTING SCIENTIFIC SPECULATION

Scientific views on the origins of HIV have shifted many times, as new evidence has been revealed, evaluated and refined — each new twist raising almost as many questions as it answers. Determining the cause and origin of any new infectious disease is a complex investigative task, which requires co-operation across many branches of biological, medical and social science. Firm conclusions take a long time to arrive.

Scientific discussions on the way to such conclusions are largely preliminary suppositions or educated guesses, rather than mature statements of fact. Media reporting of scientists' latest, most newsworthy musings, without full consideration of the background, can blur the distinction between what is known and what is only suspected.

The journalist's task in reporting on the origins of the AIDS virus has been unusually difficult, and the international media have not always precisely distinguished between speculation and evidence. The scientists themselves have also been careless at times, some perhaps influenced by the race for lucrative AIDS research contracts available in some developed countries. In the battle for research grants, the prizes sometimes seem to go to those whose ideas on the origins of AIDS are the most dramatic, most often-stated and most well-reported.

THE ORIGINS OF EPIDEMIC DISEASES: THE CASE OF SYPHILIS

We may never discover the origins of the HIV virus, just as we still do not know the origins of a sudden and virulent epidemic of syphilis which appeared in Europe in the 1490s, and raged for much of the next century. Five hundred years later, science remains uncertain where and how it started.

Until the widespread use of antibiotics in the 1940s, syphilis was feared almost as much as AIDS is today; like AIDS, it was sexually-transmitted, could lie dormant for years, and could lead to a singularly unpleasant death.

The new and frightening outbreak of syphilis seems first to have appeared in Italy. By 1495 it was in France, Germany and Switzerland; it reached Holland and Greece in 1496; it was in England and Scotland in 1497, and in Hungary and Russia in 1499.

Then, as now with AIDS, there was furious debate on the origins of the new disease. Then, as now, foreigners were usually blamed - especially foreigners who were particularly disliked. So the Russians blamed it on the Poles, and both the English and the Turks called it the French disease. The French called it the Italian illness, and the Italians called it the Spanish disease. The Spanish called it the sickness of Hispaniola, believing it to have come from what is now Haiti when Columbus returned from his voyage to the Americas.[27]

Scientists still argue about the origins of the fifteenth and sixteenth century syphilis epidemic, and with the discovery that the disease leaves tell-tale signs in bones, even in fossil bones, the story has gone further and further back in time. Did European explorers take syphilis to the New World, or did New World peoples give it to the European colonisers? Did mankind become infected with syphilis in Asia 5,000 years ago with the development of large cities, or in Africa 100,000 years ago, or have humans had syphilis since their evolution from apes?

This may help to explain why less than a decade's acquaintance with AIDS is too little to allow reliable statements about the origins of HIV. But what are the main theories?[28]

THE THREE AIDS-ORIGIN THEORIES

There are three main theories for the origins of the HIV virus: that it has developed from an old human disease not known to science; that it has developed from a natural virus disease of some other species, probably of monkeys or apes; and that it was deliberately or accidentally manufactured in a laboratory.

◆

The first theory is that HIV has been around among mankind for a very long time, and that we have not noticed it — perhaps because it has been confined to very few people, or perhaps because it has recently become more virulent. One possibility is that the disease comes from a small and isolated ethnic group, which had acquired an immunity to it so that it rarely caused death. When it spread outside this group, and reached people who had no such immunity, it became a killer.

This theory is possible: diseases familiar in one part of the world, when carried to "virgin" territory, have often proved a mortal danger to the newly exposed population. European diseases such as measles and smallpox virtually wiped out some North American Indian peoples in the eighteenth and nineteenth centuries, and isolated ethnic groups in, for example, Amazonia, can today still be ravaged by influenza. This theory is important for a key reason: if this *were* the origin of the HIV virus, then the isolated group's immunity might enable a vaccine to be developed to protect the rest of the world.

There are few completely isolated peoples left in the world, mainly in the rainforests of New Guinea, Amazonia and, perhaps, Central Africa. Since one of the early locations of AIDS was Central Africa, much speculation was focused on this possibility. By its nature this is a theory which is very difficult to disprove, but there is some evidence which argues against it.

◆

The second theory is that HIV has existed for a long time as an animal disease, and has only recently managed to infect and trigger an epidemic in humans. There are other examples of diseases "crossing over" from an animal to mankind, and since a rather similar virus to HIV has been found in a species of monkey, this possibility has received considerable attention. But in 1988 the scientists who thought they had isolated a virus similar to HIV, from wild African green monkeys, announced they had made a mistake.

◆

The third theory is that HIV is a man-made virus, perhaps from a germ warfare laboratory. Unlike the first two, this is not a scientific theory posed in terms which are open to experimental confirmation or rebuttal and presented for scrutiny in scientific journals. Rather it has been propagated like a rumour campaign with different versions picked up and relayed in various newspapers and magazines around the world.

All three theories will be discussed more fully in this and the next chapter. As we shall see, the germ warfare theory seems very unlikely indeed, and there are serious holes to be picked in the other theories too.

As Zambia's president, Dr Kenneth Kaunda, has said, it is more important to know where AIDS is going than where it has come from, and the debate about HIV's origins is largely irrelevant to immediate action against the disease.[29] The linkage of origins and blame constitutes a persistent "infection" of the international dialogue and action which is necessary to combat the spread of AIDS, and creates friction, conflict and delay.

When, if ever, a full explanation for the origins of AIDS is revealed, this may help efforts to control it. But the World Health Organization and most specialists in this field agree that AIDS prevention is not dependent on such an explanation.[30]

THE HAITIAN CONNECTION

Two parts of the developing world, Haiti and Africa, have received widespread publicity as the possible birthplace of AIDS. Haiti, a Caribbean nation whose people are racially of African descent, was singled out first.

In mid-1982, the US Centers for Disease Control — the federal public health laboratory — published a new piece of information on the mysterious disease which had already killed nearly 100 US homosexual men, and infected nearly 200 more. In just over a year, said CDC, five US states had reported 34 cases of the new illness in Haitian patients. Thirty of the 34 were men, who denied homosexual activity or drug use. Was this a new clue to the nature of the disease? CDC alerted physicians with Haitian patients to "be aware that opportunistic infections may occur in this population".[31] CDC had soon defined Haitians, along with homosexual and bisexual men, haemophiliacs, and intravenous drug users, as a "high-risk" group for AIDS. By mid-1983, this view was under attack by Haitian physicians working in the United States. Since Haitians made up only 6% of the 1,220 reported AIDS cases, and any other US ethnic group could have made up a similar or greater percentage of the total, why were Haitians being singled out, the Haitian doctors asked?[32]

The CDC argued that Haitian AIDS patients were indeed a special risk group because they had no other identifiable risk factors. But this, contended the Haitian doctors, was because Haitian men were normally reluctant to admit to homosexual activity or to intravenous drug use. The problem was not the lack of other risk factors, but the unfamiliarity of non-Haitian American researchers with Haitian attitudes toward these matters. A US physician who had worked in Haiti wrote to the UK medical journal *the Lancet*: "To admit one's homosexuality is difficult enough in America: in a country like Haiti...homosexuality or homosexual prostitution will remain a deeply hidden secret".[33]

More sensitive interviewing of patients could have revealed the true risk factors involved, said the Haitian doctors. Dr Jean-Claude Compas, vice president of the Association of Haitian Physicians Abroad and co-chairman of the Haitian Coalition on AIDS, told a US congressional committee: "Most of the data used by the CDC and other health authorities were gathered by hospital-based physicians with no knowledge of French or Creole" (the version of French spoken in Haiti), and who have admitted "a complete ignorance of Haitian culture".[34]

The categorisation of Haitians, with homosexuals and drug addicts, in a separate "risk group" was, says Dr Jean Pape, one of Haiti's leading AIDS researchers, "a serious error in the interpretation of the epidemiological data. The CDC never wondered why 88% of the early Haitian AIDS cases in the US occurred in males. In 1983 our group had identified risk factors, bisexuality and blood transfusion, in 79% of Haitian AIDS patients".[35]

"In the annals of medicine", claimed the coalition's other co-chairman, Dr Robert Auguste, "this categorisation of a nationality as a group at risk is unique".[36]

Whether or not CDC's action was justified by the very limited evidence available at the time, it became firmly accepted by the US medical world that Haitians were indeed specially at risk from AIDS, and more or less scientific speculation started as to why this might be so. Further, it became a common assumption that AIDS might have originated in Haiti, and spread from there to the United States.

Some US researchers proposed that AIDS began with an outbreak of African swine fever in Haitian pigs, and that the swine virus had been passed to humans. Others suggested that a Haitian homosexual may have contracted the swine virus from eating undercooked pork, and then passed it on to homosexual partners from the United States during acts of prostitution.[37] Another idea was that animal sacrifice and other voodoo rituals could explain the origins of human infection.[38] Others proposed that Haitians may have contracted the virus from monkeys as part of bizarre sexual practices in Haitian brothels. The possibility that AIDS arose from a disease of monkeys or pigs is discussed in Chapter Five.

There was little if any evidence for these ideas, but they were widely repeated in the United States and international media. By July 1983, a year after CDC's initial statement, the Haitian doctors' arguments began to have some impact, at least within the public health profession, and the New York City Health Commission removed Haitians from its list of risk groups for AIDS.[39]

But not until May 1985, nearly three years after its initial statement, did CDC officially withdraw its view.[40] Even then, Haitians still felt they were being officially victimised by the US authorities. "When the CDC removed Haitians from the list of risk groups, it refused to admit it had made an error," says Dr Pape. "Even now the CDC continues to stigmatise Haitians by preventing them from donating blood in the United States".

BLAMING THE HAITIANS

By 1985, the popular view that being a Haitian automatically put one at "high risk" of AIDS had caused considerable harm to Haitians, both in the United States and in Haiti. The CDC's low key report of 1982, plus the more lurid speculations on why Haitians were "high risk", was quickly translated into news stories linking Haitians in the United States with the spread of the mystery gay disease. The growing number of cases of AIDS in Haiti itself received widespread US publicity.

The second major epidemic of "blaming others" was under way following the victimisation of homosexuals. What were the results?

By 1980, between 100,000 and 300,000 Haitian refugees, fleeing the economic stagnation and political repression of the Duvalier dictatorship, had reached the United States, many sailing in rickety boats. At least half this number were living in the US illegally, for the Haitian boat people were not generally welcome, and many US immigration officials regarded as bogus the Haitians' claim to be political refugees.[41] In contrast to the thousands of Cubans who made a similar claim, the Haitians were fleeing, not a communist regime, but one supported by the US Government.

By late 1982, these immigrants, legal and illegal, found themselves officially categorised as a "risk group" for the newly-named AIDS. "Those who did not like Haitians", Reverend Gerard Jean-Juste, head of a Roman Catholic Haitian refugee centre in New York City, told the *New York Times*, "have found a new element. They are saying they do not want Haitians here because they are AIDS carriers".[42]

Haitian community workers in the United States reported that in some areas the unemployment rate for Haitians was twice that of other black workers, a situation they felt was directly attributable to AIDS. According to the AIDS Discrimination Unit of the New York City Commission on Human Rights: "Haitian children have been beaten up (and in at least one case, shot) in school; Haitian store owners have gone bankrupt as their businesses failed; and Haitian families have been evicted from their homes".[43]

Internationally, Haiti became the first Third World country to be singled out by international publicity as the possible place of origin of AIDS, and its own AIDS epidemic was placed in the international spotlight.

Haitian tourism, before 1982 the country's second largest source of foreign earnings, fell from 70,000 visitors in the winter of 1981/2 to 10,000 the following year, according to Haitian Government sources. At least six hotels had closed, with three more in financial trouble.[44] Tourism, which provided the second largest source of foreign income, has never recovered.

Haiti's tourism had indirectly supported 25,000 jobs in an economy plagued by unemployment. Since the visitors were generally from the top end of the market, the revenue was substantial. "The negative impact on our already distraught economy has been tremendous", wrote the Haitian ambassador to the United States in a September 1983 letter to the *New England Journal of Medicine*.[45]

Although the political climate in Haiti certainly bore a large share

In the United States some fringe racist organisations like the Ku Klux Klan have welcomed AIDS. Here a group in Texas in 1987 calls for homosexual men ("queers") to be interned in isolation camps. Other fringe groups have accused black men of deliberately giving AIDS to white women (see Chapter Seven). Although such groups are small, the fear and resentment they provoke can have a wider influence.

of the responsibility, knowledgeable Haitian commentators believe that the AIDS scare and not politics killed off the tourist industry.

Today, medical opinion has totally abandoned the idea that AIDS originated in Haiti. And while it seems likely that some homosexual tourists from the United States picked up the virus by having sex in Haiti, it seems equally probable that others took AIDS to Haiti and left it there.

BATTLE OF THE BLOOD TESTS: AN OLD AFRICAN DISEASE?

In 1983, at about the same time that the CDC put Haitians on the AIDS "risk group" list, Belgian and French physicians were seeing increasing numbers of immunodeficient Central African patients who came to Europe in search of treatment for their unusual malady, soon to be identified as AIDS.[46] The doctors began to suspect that AIDS might have existed for many years, unnoticed, in tropical Africa.

This was a reasonable speculation, as rare tropical diseases are sometimes carried back to developed countries. The musings of the medical profession were picked up and amplified in the press.

In one early article proposing this theory and carried in the *British Medical Journal* in August 1984, the author suggested that "...the infectious agent causing AIDS, whatever its nature, is endemic and unrecognised in parts of sub-Saharan Africa, from where it recently disseminated into external populations."[47] In the same vein a CDC virologist, Dr Donald Francis, told the *New York Times*: "I think AIDS is an old Black African disease which was introduced somewhere or other into an amplification system — for example the promiscuous segment of the homosexual community".[48]

By the end of 1985, circumstantial evidence supporting these beliefs seemed at hand. Results from the newly-developed blood test which could identify antibodies to the HIV virus were published by US researchers working on African blood samples. The samples were old ones, drawn from groups of patients in Kenya and Uganda in the 1960s and 1970s and stored for research purposes. When the American virologists tested these old samples for antibodies to the AIDS virus they got a very high percentage of positive results. In samples taken between 1980 and 1984 from the Turkana people of Kenya, for example, seemed to show that 59% were seropositive.[49] Blood samples drawn from Ugandan children in 1972-73 showed 66% to be seropositive.[50]

These "false positive" results were thought to confirm that AIDS had existed for generations, and possibly centuries, in Central Africa. The reports received widespread publicity; it has since become clear

46

that the testing technique was faulty[51] (as described in this chapter), and better tests, employing different techniques, have since been developed.[52] The researchers drew the false conclusion that infection with HIV had been widespread in Africa long before appearing in the United States or Europe. "I believe that the virus was present in Central Africa for a long period of time", Dr Robert Gallo, co-discoverer of the AIDS virus, told the *Los Angeles Times* in 1985.[53]

The implication was that the disease AIDS had also been present in Africa for a long time, unnoticed and undiagnosed by unobservant African physicians. This was considered insulting by African doctors, and does not accord with the known facts. When cases of AIDS started appearing in African hospitals, local physicians quickly recognised that a new disease was responsible, and tried to identify it. The African doctors' resentment was increased by the way that some of the early blood samples had been collected: removed from African hospitals, and tested in the United States and Europe with little or no consultation with African researchers.

There is now a strong current of opinion among scientists and others that the AIDS epidemic is as new to the African continent as it is to the rest of the world. A series of serological studies, using sensitive and specific blood tests, subject to experienced interpretation, have failed to find high prevalences of the AIDS virus in Africa before the mid-1970s, exactly the same situation as in the United States and Europe.[54] The oldest African blood sample now known to show HIV antibodies came from Kinshasa, Zaire, in 1959.[55]

On the evidence available to date, the theory that AIDS as a disease was any more widespread in Africa than it was in the United States and Europe before the 1980s appears to be a premature conclusion reached on the basis of faulty bloodtests. The political effects of this costly mistake stamped Central Africa as the birthplace of AIDS, leading to the second great epidemic of blame and counter-blame, which will be discussed in Chapter Seven.

CHAPTER FIVE

GREEN MONKEYS AND GERM WARFARE

As Chapter Four has shown, the earliest faint trace that science can find of the HIV virus is in 1959, in both Africa and the United States. There is no hard evidence for the theory that AIDS developed in Africa long before it appeared elsewhere.

In 1985 an AIDS-like virus, which was given the name STLV-3agm, was identified as having been found among wild African green monkeys. And in 1986 a second AIDS virus, named HIV-2, was found among West African people. These two developments lent new weight to speculation regarding the African origins of AIDS, and to the theory that HIV was an animal infection that had somehow been transferred to humans.

The existence of HIV-2 is not in doubt, but in early 1988 it turned out that the "discovery" of the green monkey virus named STLV-3agm was based on a laboratory error. A type of AIDS virus does infect certain monkeys in captivity, but the published evidence linking this captive monkey virus to a reservoir of viral infection in wild African monkeys was faulty. Nevertheless, the evolution of HIV from a similar ancestral virus in some mammal other than humans remains one of the possible origins of AIDS.

EVOLUTION FROM AN ANIMAL INFECTION?

From bubonic plague to malaria and yellow fever, many great human disease epidemics have been traced back to infectious organisms carried by animals or insects. Pioneering work in this field was performed by Russian scientists, for many dangerous animal infections were passed to humans when the Russians extended their agricultural operations to sparsely inhabited regions of Central Asia.[1]

Both domestic and wild animals can harbour organisms, which, when contracted by humans, can lead to an infection that in some cases

49

can be passed on from person to person independent of the original animal source. Sourcebooks written in the 1960s, before AIDS, listed 84 diseases of major significance to public health which can be transmitted from animals to humans.[2]

In some cases the human host is essential to the life cycle of the infective organism, as with the malaria parasite. Or the human may be an accidental host, contracting the infection from an animal in rare or unusual circumstances, sometimes with the result that the ensuing disease is more severe in humans than it was in the original hosts. Lassa fever, for example, is a widespread infection of rodents which does not seem to harm them, but which is serious and occasionally fatal in humans.

The story of "exotic" viruses — those which are introduced into a human society from an unusual or outside source — can be summarised, according to some medical authorities, "as the result of man's intrusion into environments in which natural selection has not fitted him to live".[3] Human invasion of a new environment, or ecological disruption of an accustomed one, may give rise to previously unknown infections. A series of such new diseases have been recognised over past decades and traced to mammalian reservoirs, often rodents or monkeys. (See Figure 5.1.)

So it is not surprising that research workers have looked among mammals for an animal reservoir for AIDS. Monkeys harbour a variety of organisms which can cause human disease, and African green monkeys are known to have acted as a reservoir for the viruses causing African yellow fever and Marburg disease. A monkey origin for AIDS is often called the "simian theory", simian being a scientific term for apes and monkeys.

There are a number of ways in which an animal disease organism can infect humans: by flea bites (which is how plague is transferred from rats), or by eating uncooked animal flesh (as with trichinosis in undercooked pork), for example. Since AIDS is a sexually transmitted disease, the theory that it originated among monkeys has in some cases given rise to the idea that the original transmission from monkey to humans was via sexual intercourse. While medical researchers have not suggested this, the idea has been repeated in some Western publications.

Many Africans have found this suggestion insulting, and have reacted strongly against the whole simian origins theory. Since the Western media dominate the international media, and since African scientists find it much harder to have their ideas reported in Western media than do European and American scientists, African scientific arguments (often powerful ones) against the simian hypothesis have not become widely known.

Figure 5.1: SOME INFECTIONS WHICH CAN PASS FROM MAMMALS TO HUMANS

Argentinian Haemorrhagic Fever:
Annual outbreaks of this disease, affecting agricultural workers in Argentina, have been traced to rodent populations which are most abundant during the maize harvest.

Izumi Fever:
Appears in sporadic outbreaks in Japan, where it was first described in 1927. It is thought that water may be contaminated by the urine or faeces of infected rodents.

Kyasanur Forest Disease:
Appeared in 1957 in Mysore state, India, as an epidemic in humans which coincided with a high death rate among forest monkeys in the region.

Lassa Fever:
A species of rat has been shown to act as a reservoir for the virus causing Lassa fever, a disease which was first noted in Nigeria in 1970.

Marburg Fever:
Appeared in Germany and Yugoslavia in 1967 among people who had handled the blood, organs or tissues of vervet monkeys from Africa, although there is no evidence of illness among the monkey trappers in the region of Uganda where the 'Marburg' monkeys were collected.

Rabies:
Native to a number of wild animals including foxes, wolves, jackals and bats. Also affects domestic dogs and cats. It is spread to humans via saliva from the bite of a rabid animal and is virtually 100% lethal unless prompt vaccination follows infection.

Rift Valley Fever:
Severe disease of cattle and sheep in East and South Africa. In 1974-5 when large numbers of animals were affected in South Africa, the first humans — farm workers and veterinarians — were infected and several died. Spreading to Egypt, the epidemic affected 100,000 people.

Yellow Fever:
Blood tests show that forest monkeys in Central and South America and in Africa could act as a reservoir of the yellow fever virus, with sporadic outbreaks of human disease occurring adjacent to forest areas. When carried to urban areas, the yellow fever virus can cause major epidemics, such as that which killed thousands of Nigerians in 1987.

The difficulty which African scientists have found in presenting their arguments internationally has reinforced a widespread African view that that Western scientists and media are deliberately blaming AIDS on Africa for racist reasons.

There seems little doubt that some Western views on the subject are motivated, deliberately or unconsciously, by racial biases. And there is no doubt whatever that Africans widely believe this to be the case. A book published in England in 1987 by a Zimbabwean social scientist and an Australian doctor illustrates this well. Theories of a monkey origin for AIDS, argue the authors, "cohabit easily with racist notions that Africans are evolutionarily closer to sub-human primates, or with images gleaned from Tarzan movies of Africans living in trees like monkeys".[4]

THE MONKEY VIRUSES

The simian theory of the origin of AIDS is that HIV arose in Africa, perhaps in the 1950s, when an ancestral virus crossed from green monkeys to humans. The evidence for this theory, part of which has been retracted by the scientists concerned, consists of genetic analysis of viruses isolated since 1985 from green monkeys and humans in West Africa, and from macaque monkeys in US laboratories.

It is confusing to talk of "the AIDS virus", because there are now two separate viruses which have been connected with AIDS: HIV-1 and HIV-2.

HIV-1 is associated with epidemics in central, east and southern Africa, in North and South America, Europe and the rest of the world. (HIV-1 was formerly called HTLV-3 by US scientists, and LAV-1 by French scientists.) HIV-1 leads to AIDS in half or more of the people it infects.

HIV-2 is often called the second AIDS virus, and was originally named LAV-2 by its French discoverers. It has been isolated from both healthy and AIDS-affected people in several West African countries. It is not yet known whether HIV-2 will cause an AIDS epidemic in West Africa of similar magnitude to that caused in central Africa and the rest of the world by HIV-1. Doctors have not yet been able to establish whether AIDS patients infected by HIV-2 will suffer the same clinical progression as those infected by HIV-1. Epidemiological evidence lends support to the belief that the HIV-2 epidemic is quite recent, and only time will tell how it will develop.

The HIV-1 and HIV-2 viruses are related, but not closely, differing by 50% of their genetic sequence. HIV-1 has no known close relatives among other viruses. But HIV-2 is about 80% similar genetically to a virus found in laboratory monkeys in California.

Early in 1983 a primate research centre in California reported four outbreaks of an AIDS-like disease in captive Asian macaque and rhesus monkeys. The earliest of the outbreaks was retrospectively diagnosed to have occurred in 1969.[5] Later the sick macaques, which came from Asia, were found to be carrying a virus similar to HIV-1, (which was given the name STLV-3mac — *mac* for macaque).[6]

Two US scientists, Phyllis Kanki and Max Essex from Harvard University, decided to try to trace HIV-1 and the macaque virus back to a common reservoir in wild monkeys. When no similar virus could be found among wild Asian macaques, they reasoned that the source of the California macaques' infection could have been a virus carried by cage-mates of a different species or place of origin. Green monkeys from Africa had shared cages with the macaques in California, and since AIDS had already appeared in Africa but not in Asia, Kanki and Essex selected wild-caught African green monkeys for their research.

In 1985 they announced that they had isolated a new virus, which they called STLV-3agm (*agm* for African green monkey), from wild African green monkeys, which all appeared healthy and unaffected.[7] So it seemed as if wild green monkeys could indeed be the source of the AIDS-like virus which had infected macaques in California.

Could the same green monkey virus also be the source of human AIDS? Collaborating this time with French and Senegalese scientists, Kanki and Essex decided to look for evidence of such infection in Senegal, West Africa.[8] In 1986 this international team announced that all the blood samples they had taken from apparently healthy Senegalese people contained antibodies which reacted strongly with STLV-3agm, the virus carried by African green monkeys. The virus isolated from these people was named HTLV-4.

So an intriguing and plausible theory grew up. The green monkey virus STLV-3agm, which did not seem to cause disease, might be the original source of AIDS. Somehow, it had infected West African people, changing slightly into HTLV-4, but still not causing any noticeable disease. HTLV-4 then evolved into HIV-2, which causes AIDS, and then HIV-2 evolved into HIV-1, the killer virus linked with AIDS around the world. The green monkey virus STLV-3agm, it was suggested, had also passed from green monkeys to captured macaques, becoming the virus STLV-3, which had caused AIDS-like symptoms in the captive macaques in California and labelled STLV-3mac.

When it was first proposed, many virologists found this theory attractive. But they started to become suspicious in April 1987, when a second group of Harvard researchers published a comparison of the genetic material of these various virus samples. The two viruses discovered by Kanki and Essex — STLV-3agm from the African green monkeys, and HTLV-4 from Senegalese people — plus STLV-3mac from the Californian macaques *all* proved to be genetically virtually identical.

The second Harvard group commented that it was "startling" to see such close similarity in viruses infecting three different species: two monkey species and humankind. Normally, when a virus crosses over from one host species to another, it undergoes substantial genetic changes.

One obvious explanation was laboratory contamination. Perhaps the virus isolates from blood samples of African green monkeys and Senegalese people had become contaminated by the macaque virus? This sort of contamination is not unusual, and virologists regularly exercise elaborate care to avoid it. Had something gone wrong in Kanki and Essex's lab at Harvard?

THE PHANTOM VIRUS

Kanki and Essex rechecked their results, and early in 1988 announced that contamination must have occurred. Their two new viruses, STLV-3agm from green monkeys, and HTLV-4 from Senegalese people, originated not in West Africa but in laboratory cultures of the macaque or another captive monkey virus. It is to their credit that they openly acknowledged this, but their announcement has thrown public understanding of research into the origins of the AIDS virus into some confusion. STLV-3agm has proved to be a phantom, but there *is* a monkey virus. The question now is: where did it come from?

Scientific research, speculation and guesswork on the relationship between these various viruses has been filling the world's scientific journals, and will continue to do so. At least three other groups of scientists, in the United States, Germany and Japan, say they have isolated HIV-like viruses from African green monkeys, although by early 1988 their work had not been published. Their results have therefore not been subjected to the scientific scrutiny which eventually discredited the work of Kanki and Essex.

So did HIV-1, the virus which causes AIDS, evolve from an animal virus? In October 1987, before Kanki and Essex's retraction had been published, leading French virologist Luc Montagnier suggested to *Le Monde*: "All these viruses have a common centre, or origin, which remains to be discovered. The arguments in favour of an African origin are in reality very weak. To determine the exact source of the present AIDS pandemic we must search for this common point of origin in other parts of the world."[9]

The chance remains that the AIDS virus may be descended from an animal virus found somewhere other than Africa. The macaque virus itself must have come from somewhere, and although cage-mate green monkeys and other cage-mate monkeys were one potential source, it is possible that captive macaques contracted their AIDS virus in the wild from their Asian troupe-mates. But so far tests on wild Asian macaques have failed to turn up the virus.

It has been widely considered in Africa that the green monkey theory has become popular at least partly because Westerners wish to "blame" Africans for starting the AIDS epidemic. And after the Kanki and Essex episode, any new theories which propose Africa as the birthplace of AIDS will be regarded with extreme scepticism in many parts of the Third World.

"There is a lack of rigour in the simian origins theory taken as a whole which, I think, has been considered more acceptable since the finger is pointing at Africa than would have been the case if it had pointed somewhere else — at the United States, for example," says Professor Abib Samb, head of the Department of Virology and Bacteriology in the University of Dakar's Faculty of Medicine.

Because African scientific views on the origins of AIDS are not widely publicised, Panos asked Professor Samb, together with two colleagues at the Senegal-based non-governmental environment and development organisation, ENDA (Environnement et Développement du Tiers Monde), to analyse the African green monkey hypothesis. Their conclusion was written in late 1987, before the withdrawal of the Kanki and Essex claims to have discovered two new viruses. It is that this hypothesis, while not impossible, is "no more plausible than flying saucers".

FLYING SAUCERS AND THE MONKEY VIRUS

BY
Philippe Engelhard, ENDA, Dakar
Professor Abib Samb, University of Dakar
Moussa Seck, ENDA, Dakar

Some scientists today believe that the family of viruses responsible for the global AIDS epidemic are probably of African origin, transmitted to humans from monkeys. A certain amount of evidence which could support this hypothesis has been presented — but is the hypothesis itself consistent, logical and persuasive? In order for it to stand up, those proposing this hypothesis need to demonstrate that:

— there are one or more monkey viruses which are related to the human AIDS virus;

— that the virus causing AIDS in humans is either so closely related to the monkey virus that the link between the two is inescapable; or that the human AIDS virus is a mutation of the monkey virus, in which case it must be shown how the mutation altered the virus' genetic structure to make it so harmful in humans.

— that there exist modes of transmission of the monkey virus to humans which are biologically, culturally and ecologically credible;

— that the AIDS virus which infects people on continents other than Africa is the AIDS virus most closely related to the African monkey virus;

— that the African origin of the AIDS virus family is unique, and that there do not exist in other places other animal reservoirs of viruses which could give rise to AIDS in humans;

Even if they could meet these logical requirements (and few of them have so far been met), proponents of the monkey-to-man hypothesis would still have to satisfy certain conditions of plausibility. Allowing for the moment that acceptable modes of transmission between monkeys and humans in Africa can be demonstrated, it is logical that African populations ecologically closest to the monkeys in question should have been infected by virus(es) of the AIDS family for longer than people elsewhere, because more frequent opportunities for infection would have been present. Such lengthy infection in these populations has not been demonstrated. On the contrary, such data as exists leads in the opposite direction,[10] showing little evidence of infection in Central, East and West Africa prior to 1975. Longstanding infection cannot be ruled out, but even pygmies, who live in closest proximity to monkeys, show seropositivity only where there has been sexual contact with outsiders.[11] It is true that peoples living in the green monkey range eat monkey, usually stewed or roasted. This constitutes a very small risk of transmission, in our view, since the virus is very heat-sensitive. Even if it were not destroyed in cooking, it would be unlikely to survive the rigours of the digestive tract, so eating infected monkey does not appear to be a plausible route of transmission. Monkey bites do not seem a likely alternative, in view of the small quantity of virus likely to be present in saliva. More exotic means of transmission could be posited, but on the whole their probability seems very low.

Nor has AIDS itself been shown to be common among these groups. It might be suggested that rural groups exposed to the monkey virus have some form of natural immunity to the AIDS virus. If so, why would this immunity have so little apparent damping effect on the spread of the infection, in rural and urban areas?

AIDS in Africa broke out suddenly, in cities, about the same time as it appeared in the United States and Haiti. The pattern of spread of AIDS in Africa is precisely *not* what the monkey hypothesis would lead us to expect. Is there then an additional "X" factor which could account for the geographic and temporal shape of the AIDS epidemic in Africa? The monkey-to-man theory is based on a chain of unverified assumptions: that the monkey virus suddenly mutated to become an AIDS virus, infecting rural individuals who then migrated to the city where they passed on their new infection to promiscuous individuals, from whom it spread rapidly into the sexually active age group, and thence back into some rural areas.

Or perhaps, as some have claimed, the monkey virus is an ancient infection in humans which metamorphosed into an AIDS virus and took hold in the cities during the post-colonial upsurge of rural to urban migration. If this were true, we would expect old people in rural areas from which migration to AIDS-affected cities took place to show high levels of AIDS virus infection — but available data indicate that they show no infection at all. [12]

While urbanisation might, under certain circumstances, explain the dispersion of the AIDS virus, it does not account for the proposed mutation. The appearance of this mutation is critical for the suggested chain of assumptions, yet, to our knowledge, convincing arguments to show exactly how it could have happened have not been made.

One way that monkey theorists could explain the epidemic spread of AIDS in African cities would be to suggest that African populations are more vulnerable than others to the AIDS virus. Were this the case, however, it would suggest that Africans lacked resistance to the AIDS virus, and that it was therefore not of African origin — exactly the reverse of what they suppose.

A central weakness of their hypothesis derives from the existence of two AIDS viruses: HIV-1, associated with AIDS in Central Africa and the rest of the world, and HIV-2, associated less strongly with AIDS in West Africa. HIV-2 seems to be very closely related to a virus carried by green monkeys*. HIV-1, the virus responsible for most of the world's AIDS cases, is only a very distant cousin of the monkey virus.

The key piece of experimental evidence which would show the derivation of HIV-1 from the African monkey virus*, thus demonstrating the African origins of AIDS, is non-existent. It is just possible that HIV-1 could have mutated from the monkey virus*, but this seems very unlikely. Thus, though the territorial range of the African monkey more or less matches the region worst affected by AIDS, the virus rampant in this area is HIV-1, making the simian hypothesis for the origin of AIDS seem frankly paradoxical. It is regrettable that such a vague geographical coincidence gave rise to this hypothesis.

An alternative hypothesis, that of the passage of a simian virus to humans on another continent, has as far as we know not been seriously investigated. It is the examination and rejection of alternative hypotheses which gives any surviving hypothesis its scientific credibility. We are forced to the view that with respect to the simian hypothesis for the African origin of AIDS, scientific rigour continues to be a low priority.

Defenders of the simian hypothesis are forced to invoke a large number of "ad hoc" hypotheses in order to bolster their primary claim for the African origin of the AIDS virus. Their hypothesis is neither clear nor compelling. Though it has yet to be refuted, it is no more plausible than flying saucers. Just as the AIDS virus is fragile when exposed to heat and air, so this hypothesis, in our view, withers on exposure to rigorous scientific scrutiny.

* *Since this contribution was written, the existence of the green monkey virus named STLV-3agm has been shown to have been based on a laboratory error: see discussion earlier in this chapter.*

MONKEY-RESEARCH: THE ROADS NOT TAKEN

"Based on the evidence available," says Philippe Engelhard of ENDA in Dakar, "we are not in a position to explain the outbreak of the AIDS epidemic in Africa. [But] many of the suppositions which have been used to glue the simian hypothesis together could apply, strictly speaking, to the alternative hypothesis that AIDS began in the United States or in other centres."

Scientists have not constructed such an alternative theory because, some critics say, they "found it so difficult to imagine that white people could infect Africans with AIDS and not the reverse".[13]

If an ancestral AIDS virus did exist in monkeys, how would it have passed to humans? Some researchers have suggested that as "African green monkeys are somewhat gregarious and are regarded as agricultural pests", a monkey bite could have transmitted the virus from animal to man.[14] An alternative hypothesis could be that an infected captive monkey in a US primate establishment could have bitten a handler or keeper.

Mutation of the monkey virus, if it did occur, could just as easily have happened in the United States, where the rapid partner-change among homosexual men, in San Francisco and other cities, provided ideal circumstances for rapid multiplication of the infection. The global spread of AIDS, critics of the African simian origin would argue, is more consistent with the assumption that affluent, mobile US homosexual men were the earliest carriers of the AIDS virus than monkey-bitten African peasants.

Italian virologists have suggested that the opportunities for transmission of an AIDS virus from monkeys to humans may have increased with the rise, in the 1950s, of the large-scale trade in monkeys from Africa to Western countries to meet new demands in medical research.[15] This argument could apply to anyone, African or non-African, involved in the trade and handling of infected monkeys. On the basis of retrospective blood analyses, African green monkeys have been reported to carry antibodies to the macaque AIDS-like virus as early as 1957-62.[16]

From the 1950s African green monkey tissues have been used extensively for biomedical research. Much of the oral polio vaccine used throughout the world since 1954 is produced on cultures of kidney cells taken from green monkeys. Risk of infection could have been present for scientists and technicians involved in the killing and dissection of these monkeys and in the preparation of the tissues for research. The organism causing Marburg disease in staff in European laboratories in 1967 is thought to have been picked up in just this way by personnel who handled the blood, organs or tissues of African vervet monkeys.

ARMCHAIR ANTHROPOLOGY?

Just as some African scientists are critical of the apparent lack of interest by Western scientific researchers in seeking an origin of AIDS outside Africa, so they also criticise the wealth of non-scientific conjecture concerning African cultural practices which might have led to the passage of a monkey virus to humans. These critics have given several examples of what might be called "armchair anthropology". One such instance is the suggestion advanced by British authors in 1986: "Monkeys are often hunted for food in Africa. Once caught, monkeys are often kept in huts for some time before they are eaten. Dead monkeys are often used as toys by African children".[17]

Before African monkeys became the focus of such speculations, Haitian pigs were the object of similar guesswork about the possible origins of AIDS. In a 1983 letter to a prominent medical journal, a Harvard researcher suggested that the AIDS virus could be a mutation of the virus which causes a disease in pigs known as African swine fever. The letter noted that an outbreak of swine fever occurred in Haiti in 1978/9, just before the first appearance of AIDS in Haiti, and claimed that swine fever broke out in Cuba just after numbers of Haitian refugees arrived there in 1980. The origin of AIDS, suggested the author, might be traced to the eating of undercooked pork from pigs infected with the swine fever virus by Haitian homosexuals, who then spread the virus in Haiti and the United States.[18] Though the swine fever hypothesis was quickly rejected by virologists, it was kept alive for several years by homosexual publications in New York.[19]

More bizarre hypotheses have been published. A recent theory can be traced back to 1973, well before the advent of AIDS, when a Zairean anthropologist published the results of his fieldwork with peoples living in the Great Lakes region of Africa. His 214-page book examined the family life, and culture and sexual practices of these peoples, and in the chapter on sexual life appeared the brief statement that "to stimulate a man or woman, and to induce in them intense sexual activity, they are inoculated in the thighs, pubic region and back with blood taken from the male monkey (for a man) or the female monkey (for a woman)".[20]

Fourteen years later, in June 1987, the British medical journal *The Lancet* published a letter from F. Noireau, an anthropologist working with the French research organisation ORSTOM in Brazzaville in the Congo. Noireau drew the attention of *Lancet* readers to the possibility that the inoculation of monkey blood described by Kashamura might have provided a mechanism for the transfer of an AIDS virus from monkeys to humans.[21]

This possible mechanism for the transmission of the AIDS virus from monkeys to humans was repeated two weeks later in the British weekly popular science magazine, *New Scientist,* which published an article by Abraham Karpas, a University of Cambridge medical researcher working on AIDS. He warned that some European physicians who sometimes injected their patients with "monkey glands" might run similar risks.[22]

The original observation by the Zairean anthroplogist, not made in connection with AIDS, has been widely repeated since by nonanthropologists[23], to demonstrate the feasibility of monkey-to-human transmission of the AIDS virus. Africans tend to regard such accounts as far-fetched, but as Kenyan journalist, Wanume Kibedi, comments, "many in the end gain the ring of truth simply because they are repeated often enough".[24]

It must be said that viruses have in the past crossed over from animals to humans, and the mechanisms they have used must be unusual and rare for the cross-over not to have occurred earlier. Nevertheless, many African scientists have resented Europeans and North Americans, many of them patently ignorant of conditions in Africa, evaluating the likelihood of this or that suggested mechanism.

AIDS ORIGINS: WHY DOESN'T THE UNITED STATES LOOK AT HOME?

Again and again, in Third World criticisms of Western AIDS research and media coverage, the question is asked: why has there been so little investigation of the possibility that the AIDS virus originated in the United States? After all, roughly 65% of the world's reported AIDS cases are found there. Is not the fact that almost no research has been devoted to this question in itself evidence of a Western bias against the Third World in general and Africa in particular? Epidemiology, Third Worlders say, should begin at home.

Conspicuous by its absence, these critics point out, is the "missing hypothesis" — one which would send researchers in pursuit of the earliest evidence of the AIDS virus in stored *US* blood samples, and which would attempt to trace the spread of the virus *from* the United States *to* the rest of the world.

The asymmetry in AIDS "origins" research has left a breach into which conspiracy theories can march. If Africans often see in Western discussion of an African origin of AIDS a wish to blame the epidemic on Africa, so many Third Worlders have found attractive a counter-blame theory: that AIDS was unleashed on the world by germ warfare experimentation in the US Defense Department laboratory at Fort Detrick, Maryland.[25]

AIDS AS A US MILITARY CONSPIRACY

In 1986 three East German scientists produced a paper on which the details of this argument, taken up by newspapers in many parts of the world, have been based.[26] The article, which is believed to have first circulated in September of that year, made a purely speculative case. HIV is an unusual type of virus known as a retrovirus; two other retroviruses, one which attacks sheep and the other which infects humans, could have been combined to create a virus with the properties of HIV, suggested the paper.

A July 1987 US State Department report[27] exhaustively argues that the Fort Detrick hypothesis was launched as part of a Soviet disinformation campaign designed to discredit the United States in

*The theory that AIDS was created in a US laboratory has proved popular in many countries. Top left is a cartoon from the Soviet publication **Pravda**, 30 October 1986, reproduced in a US Department of State publication; it shows a Pentagon scientist handing a soldier the AIDS virus in return for money. The headline top right is from Nigeria, (**The African Interpreter**, October 1986). The headline at the bottom is from Costa Rica: "Claim made that AIDS was created in the United States" (**Semanario Universidad**, 3 April 1987).*

advance of international arms control negotiations centred on biological weapons.

The State Department report records that in September 1986, during the summit of the Non-aligned Movement in Harare, Zimbabwe, a Zimbabwean magazine published an article based on the East German claims entitled "AIDS: USA homemade evil; not imported from

Africa".[28]   A month later a Nigerian news journal published an unsigned review of the East German paper stressing the "remarkable correlation between the establishment of the first military institution devoted to gene manipulation of viruses in 1977, and the first registered cases of AIDS in New York".[29]   An Indian magazine followed in February 1987 with "AIDS, a US military monster: Yankee business, not monkey business", [30] an interview with one of the East Germans which was picked up by journals in Nairobi and Senegal in June and July.[31]

A Ghanaian daily newspaper in April 1987 charged that US medical personnel were conducting "intensive experiments" with the AIDS virus in Zaire, Argentina and Pakistan,[32] while a Nicaraguan daily alleged in July 1987 that the United States was using AIDS as a "bacteriological weapon" to "halt the [population] growth" of Latin American and Asian countries.[33]

At the third international conference on AIDS in Washington in June 1987, an ad hoc group called the United Front Against Racism and Capitalism-Imperialism distributed a broadsheet, which it claimed was based on "exhaustive research, study and analysis of over 300 scientific and medical papers", which said that AIDS was "germ warfare by the US Government against gays and blacks".

A number of virologists in the United States and Europe dismissed the East German paper. According to Dr David Katzenstein, an American virologist working in Zimbabwe, it was "poor science", and "based on a series of assumptions which have been shown by a large number of people, not all Americans and including some Africans, to be incorrect".[34]   Dr Richard Tedder, a virologist involved in AIDS research at the Middlesex Hospital Medical School in London, saw the theory as "implausible and without a scientific foundation".[35] Professor Luc Montagnier, co-discoverer of the AIDS virus, regarded the theory as "not serious enough to even raise the hypothesis".[36]

The US State Department may or may not be correct that the original East German paper was a disinformation plot by Soviet intelligence. But Soviet scientists have themselves joined the ranks of those rejecting the germ warfare theory. "Not a single [Soviet] scientist has even hinted that AIDS was artificially manufactured," a leading Soviet academician told a press conference in Moscow in October 1987, "and the Soviet Academy of the Sciences has never had anything to do with such accusations".[37] The Soviet daily *Izvestia* published an article by two scientists on the same day in which they criticised the Soviet press for spreading the false US laboratory origins theory. [38]

Like all conspiracy theories, AIDS-as-germ-warfare is impossible to disprove, but it does seem improbable. The first argument against it is that genetic engineering was not sufficiently advanced to develop such a man-made virus at the time HIV first appeared. The AIDS virus must have been in existence several years before 1980, when widespread cases of AIDS started to appear in US hospitals; if one accepts the evidence for AIDS cases as early as 1959 it must have been in existence since the mid-1950s. Virologists are emphatic that even if such a virus could be developed today, the science of genetic engineering was not sufficiently advanced in the late 1970s for this to be possible.

The second argument is that a virus like HIV is not the sort of bug a germ warfare laboratory would wish to develop. There is no point in developing a virus as a weapon unless one's own side can be protected against it. The ideal germ warfare organism would be one that caused disease very quickly, that did not spread by itself but only infected those deliberately infected with it, and for which there was a vaccine to be used to protect one's own side. The HIV virus differs from this profile in every respect.

Few if any virologists take seriously the theory that HIV is the result of a scientific conspiracy. So far there is no substantive evidence whatever that this is where AIDS came from, while there are a number of convincing arguments that this origin is unlikely in the extreme.

In any case, even if the US germ warfare theory of AIDS were true, it is difficult to see how it could ever be verified. Anyone who believes that the US military deliberately developed the HIV virus, and unleashed it on the world to exterminate homosexuals and blacks, is likely also to believe that the military will by now have silenced all those involved in the original research. Like all conspiracy theories, this one is hard to refute.

One of the main attractions of the theory is undoubtedly that it blames the United States for AIDS. It has appeared repeatedly in Third World newspapers, by authors who view the US debate over the possible African origins of AIDS as evidence of racism and a determination to blame Africans.

BLAMING OTHERS

The tendency to blame other peoples and other races for the AIDS epidemic will be documented further in Chapter Seven. Of course, not all or even many of those who support any one origins theory are motivated by racism, or a desire to blame others. But this element is certainly a strand which runs through the debate.

"Origins" research will continue, for at least two reasons. First, it could provide a clue to developing a vaccine against HIV, without which AIDS cannot be eradicated. (This does not alter the fact that the origin of AIDS is irrelevant to prevention by the only methods we have at present: by protecting blood supplies, and by sexual education.)

Second, scientific curiosity will guarantee that research will continue to try and resolve the mystery of where this new and unusual virus came from. It seems probable that a virus to HIV will eventually be found among some wild animal population, or some isolated human ethnic group; at present it is difficult to see another likely explanation.

So the origins debate will go on; it is one of the hottest scientific issues of the 1980s. It is probably optimistic to hope that it will be conducted without continuing imputations of blame, and without a continuing belief by others that blame is being imputed. But scientists, media and politicians alike would do well to exercise great restraint in this discussion, since feelings of being blamed are already seriously hampering efforts to control AIDS.

CHAPTER SIX

SEX AND RACE

Chapters Four and Five have discussed the origins of AIDS, and have shown how this debate has become entangled with accusations of blame and counter-blame. Knowledge about the way in which AIDS spreads has become equally entangled. This chapter looks mainly at the reasons for the rapid spread of AIDS in Africa; it examines the roles of other sexually transmitted diseases, "promiscuity", prostitutes, and the possibility that susceptibility to HIV might be genetically linked. ˊ

The AIDS virus is primarily transmitted through sexual intercourse. There are two key scientific factors which allow us to understand its spread: the likelihood that an infected person will transmit the virus to a partner during sexual intercourse, and the frequency with which individuals acquire new sexual partners.[1] Slowing down the spread of the virus requires both a reduction in the likelihood of its transmission during any single act of sexual intercourse, and a reduction in the rate at which new sexual partners are acquired.

SCIENCE AND MORALISING

These factors can be stated simply enough in scientific papers. But turned into layman's language, they rapidly acquire powerful emotional overtones. First, a high rate of partner change translates into everyday language as "promiscuity", regarded as more or less immoral in most societies.

Second, the likelihood that the virus will be transmitted in any act of sexual intercourse could, it appears, be increased by certain forms of sex (notably anal sex), and when one or other partner is infected with another sexually-transmitted disease (STD: often called venereal disease). Both anal sex and infection with such STDs as syphilis and gonorrhoea are also widely regarded as shameful.

Third, without thus far producing hard evidence, scientists are exploring the idea that there may be genetic factors which make some ethnic groups more vulnerable to infection by HIV than others — a possibility which has a great potential for racial disharmony.

So, as with the origins of AIDS, a discussion of the spread of HIV infection easily becomes entangled with epidemics of blame. These issues are all so loaded with cultural and religious significance that the mere mention of AIDS can in many contexts provoke anxiety, denial, or hostility. On the international front an extra, and explosive, dimension has been added — that of inter-racial friction. This element arises most commonly when the subject is AIDS in Africa.

This chapter looks first at the relationship between AIDS and STDs, particularly in Africa; it then considers the role which promiscuity plays as one factor in the spread of these diseases; and finally it examines the controversial possibility that different ethnic groups may vary in their susceptibility to AIDS.

WHY ARE STDs ON THE INCREASE?

AIDS is primarily a sexually transmitted disease (though it can also be transmitted by non-sexual means). When viewed in this way, AIDS becomes a new and more sinister manifestation of an enduring problem: that of high and rising rates of STDs, particularly in the developing world.

Long before AIDS was heard of, specialists in STDs were arguing that these infections constituted an excessive drain on health resources, especially in Africa and parts of Asia.[2] In the last two decades STDs have been many times more common in regions of the the Third World, both urban and rural, than in North America and Western Europe.[3]

The figures suggest that syphilis, genital ulcer disease, chlamydia, gonorrhoea and some other STDs may be more common in some African groups than anywhere else in the world.[4] "The general impression of many practising physicians", writes one group of African doctors, "is that the STDs, particularly gonorrhoea, may have reached endemic proportions in the urban areas of tropical Africa, with

Figure 6.1: Rates of STDs per 100,000 population (early 1970s)

	Gonorrhoea	Syphilis
Kampala	5,143	572
Nairobi	3,600	280
Greater London	308	8
Atlanta, Georgia	2,510	88

*[Source: O. P. Arya and F. J.Bennett, "Role of the medical auxiliary in the control of sexually transmitted disease in a developing country", **British Journal of Venereal Diseases**, 1976, vol 52, pp 116-21]*

increasing spread to the rural areas."[5]   So common is gonorrhoea among some ethnic groups, African doctors have written, that its symptoms are sometimes regarded as a sign of sexual awakening or potency.[6]

As Figure 6.1 shows, rates of gonorrhoea and syphilis are more than 10 times higher in Kampala and Nairobi than in London, and rates of syphilis are about 50 times higher. Even compared with Atlanta in the United States, where rates are even higher than in London, the two African cities have two to five times more STDs.

"It is obvious", according to Dr A. O. Osoba, a Nigerian STD expert, "that STDs in Africa constitute a major public health problem".[7] But while in some African regions the problem is especially acute, African countries are not alone in facing serious STD epidemics. High rates of sexual infections are found in many parts of the developing world. The World Health Organization ranks STDs among the Third World's most pressing health problems: malaria, diarrhoeal disease, malnutrition and tuberculosis.[8]

Figure 6:2   Incidence of Gonorrhoea per 100,000 population in selected countries 1971-82

	Incidence per 100,000 population
Kampala, Uganda, 1971 [1]	10,000
Uganda (rural), 1971 [1]	3,000
Nairobi, Kenya, 1971 [1]	7,000
United States, 1982 [2]	407
Costa Rica, 1982 [3]	392
Denmark, 1973 [2]	331
Sweden, 1975 [2]	300
Cuba, 1983 [3]	232
Colombia [3]	133

*[Source: 1: A. O. Osoba, "Sexually transmitted diseases in tropical Africa: a review of the present situation,"**British Journal of Venereal Diseases**, 1981, vol 57, pp 89-94; 2: **Population Reports**, July 1983, volume 11, number 3, 151 pp; 3: figures calculated from statistics presented in: Pan American Health Organization, **Health of Women in the Americas**, 1985, p 144]*

Directly comparable data, from which an accurate statistical picture of the relative seriousness of STDs in various developing countries can be built up, is non-existent. However, some comparisons can be made, and they show that while STD "hot spots" are dotted around the world, most of the dots fall in the developing countries.

Gonorrhoea is one of the most common STDs in both developed and developing countries. In the Figure 6.2 rates of gonorrhoeal infection per 100,000 population are given for countries in Africa, Europe and the Americas.

Figure 6:3 :   Comparative rates of tubal abnormalities among women in developing countries 1973-8

	No of women	% with abnormalities
Highlands,Papua New Guinea [1]	220	86
Nairobi, Kenya [2]	104	73
North Sulawesi Peninsula, Indonesia [3]	228	62
Tunisia [4]	114	56
Libreville, Gabon [5]	228	44

*[1: G. R. Campbell and K. Roberts-Thompson, **Papua New Guinea Medical Journal**, December 1974, volume 17, number 4, pp 347-533; 2: J. K. G.Mati et al, **East African Medical Journal**, February 1973, volume 50, number 50, pp 94-7]; 3: J. Barten, **Andrologica**, September- October 1978, volume 10, number 5, pp 405-12; 4: E. Gargoucha et al, **Tunisie medicale,** November- December 1976, volume 54, number 6, pp 833-36; 5: H. Moustinga, **Médecine d'Afrique Noire**, February 1973, volume 20, number 2, pp 103-9]*

One rough measure of the prevalence of STDs in a community is the frequency with which women seek medical treatment for certain reproductive disorders. Untreated sexual infections in women often cause blockages in the fallopian tubes, through which a woman's egg cell must travel on its way to implantation in the uterus.   The prevalence of such blockages among women in a population gives a very approximate indication of the degree to which STDs are a problem for that population. (Since tubal blockages have other causes, their presence is not a precise indicator of previous sexual infection.) Women whose tubes are scarred as the result of contracting an STD, and who as a result are unable to have children, are found in both developed and developing countries, but more so in the latter. Surveys of women reporting to clinics in various Third World countries indicate the comparative incidence of tubal abnormalities: see Figure 6.3.

STDs IN SUB-SAHARAN AFRICA

In developing countries, those who contract an STD are less likely to obtain effective treatment than people in North America and Europe.[9] As a result, more cases of advanced sexual infections are seen in poorer countries; in particular, secondary infertility (inability to conceive or bear children due to damage to the reproductive organs caused by an untreated STD) is common.[10] Indeed, although untreated STDs are not the *only* cause of secondary infertility, some researchers believe that secondary infertility gives a good indication of the prevalence of STDs.

Infertility caused by STDs reaches its highest known levels in parts of sub-Saharan Africa. In a 25-country World Health Organization study of infertility between 1979 and 1984, the participating African centres showed a pattern of infertility different both from developed countries and from other developing regions. African couples were more likely to have a history of STDs, and more likely to be infertile as a result.[11]

The international media has often focused on the high overall fertility rates and rapid population growth of countries like Kenya, but for many Africans, childlessness is a bigger problem. In some areas of sub-Saharan Africa, over 40% of couples of reproductive age are childless, compared with only 3% in developing countries as a whole.[12] This is believed to be mainly due to a high level of STDs.

Most of the sexually transmitted infections common in the tropics are caused by bacteria, which unlike viruses can be treated by antibiotics. But misuse of these drugs, either by inadequately trained health workers or through self-treatment, has led to the development of strains of STD bacteria-resistant to all but the newest and most expensive antibiotics.[13] In Africa, such resistant bacterial strains have been reported across the sub-Saharan region.[14] Wherever they flourish, new outbreaks of antibiotic-resistant STDs spring up, which are extremely difficult to eradicate. Some doctors argue that indiscriminate use of antibiotics is one of the chief reasons for the high prevalence of STDs in Africa.

It is important to realise that while sub-Saharan Africa's level of STDs is high compared with other regions of the world today, it is not

71

high compared to the developed world at a time when their cities were subjected to similar pressures of rapid growth, migration and social upheaval. In Boston in 1911, one study suggests that over 30% of hospital out-patients had gonorrhoeal infections[15] — a figure not dissimilar to the levels of HIV infection recorded among patients at STD clinics in parts of Central Africa in 1985- 6. In 1914 in New York City, prison health officials estimated that 75-90% of prostitutes had STDs,[16] a figure which compares with current HIV data from Rwanda and Kenya suggesting that over 80% of certain groups of prostitutes may be infected.

African researchers have for many years urged "a change of attitude of health administrators in the developing countries of tropical Africa to recognise that STDs are a serious problem and require energetic control measures".[17] But though African and other experts considered the incidence of STDs in some African cities to be "appallingly high",[18] there has been no broad-scale campaign to eradicate STDs in the sub-Sahara in over 20 years.[19]

WHY STDs HELP SPREAD AIDS

People who contract HIV very often have a history of repeated infection with other sexually-transmitted diseases. Homosexual men writing about the AIDS epidemic in their communities in New York and San Francisco have recorded how casually many gay men in the late 1970s regarded their prodigious numbers of sexual partners and their repeated bouts of all manner of STDs.[20]

A high level of STDs is clearly related to a high rate of sexual partner change, and frequent sexual partner change has undoubtedly played a role in the AIDS epidemics in Africa and the rest of the Third World, just as it did in encouraging the spread of AIDS among US and European homosexuals. But this is not the whole story in either case. Having certain other STDs makes it easier for the HIV virus to be transferred from one partner to the other during sex.

North American epidemiologists have estimated the risk of contracting HIV in a single act of unprotected heterosexual intercourse with a carrier at less than 1%.[21] Epidemiological studies in Africa[22] and the United States[23] suggest that certain other STDs can make it easier to become infected with the AIDS virus. There are two probable reasons for this. First, many STDs cause ulcers or other sores on the genitals of both men and women; these sores make it easier for the HIV virus to leave one bloodstream and enter the other. Second, when an individual has another sexually transmitted infection, the body sends lymphocytes (the white blood cells which fight disease organisms) to the genital region — and HIV lives in these cells.

This increased efficiency of HIV transmission in the presence of other STDs seems to occur regardless of the sex of the partners.[24] For homosexual men, the risk incurred appears to be increased if they engage in unprotected anal intercourse (ie without using a strong condom). Certain cells found in the lining of the rectum are highly susceptible to infection by HIV.[25] In Africa, recent epidemiological research suggests that two STDs — genital ulcers and *Chlamydia trachomatis* infection — may play a role in the transmission of HIV independent of the frequency of partner change.[26]

Genital ulcer disease and infection by HIV are frequently found in individuals with many sexual partners — low socio-economic group prostitutes, for example. So it is extremely difficult to show which came first: multiple partners leading to genital ulcers and subsequently infection with HIV, or infection with both genital ulcers and HIV as a result of multiple partners. Recent studies have sought to untangle these factors and their results\have important implications.

Women infected with genital ulcer disease or chlamydia, both of which damage the genital membranes are, according to a local study carried out in Nairobi, Kenya, much more likely to contract HIV during sexual intercourse with an infected partner, than women without such ulcers.[27] In a group of women studied in Harare, Zimbabwe, the risk of catching HIV tripled for those who had a history of genital ulcer disease.[28] Genital ulcers are themselves a result of such sexual infections as herpes, syphilis and chancroid.

Genital ulcers in men may also provide an entry point for the passage of the virus from female to male. Additionally, it seems that the presence of genital ulcers in the female sexual partner could have the effect of multiplying the risk of catching HIV for the male partner, by increasing the infectivity of the woman. One African study found that men who had had sex with a woman with genital ulcers had a 5-10% chance of contracting HIV from a single sexual exposure.[29]

By contrast, studies of couples where one partner is HIV positive as a result of blood tranfusion show that for the uninfected partner the risk of acquiring the AIDS virus is 7-23% over a period of years.[30] These figures — compared with the estimated less than 1% risk per sexual act between otherwise healthy heterosexuals in the United States — do much to explain the wide and heterosexual spread of HIV in Africa.

If the presence of another STD does make that person more likely to contract HIV during sex with an HIV carrier, then the extent to which STDs are already part of daily life for sexually active adults in Africa may help to explain the swift and sudden conquest of these same places by the AIDS virus. The World Health Organization estimates that a minimum of 10,000 Africans are progressing to AIDS each year.[31] and that a further one million are carrying the HIV virus.[32]

WHAT IS "PROMISCUITY"?

The fact that AIDS in Central Africa has spread so rapidly among heterosexuals is often said by Europeans and North Americans to be due to the much greater "promiscuity" of Africans. As with many other Western comments on AIDS in Africa, this assumption is widely resented by Africans, and often blamed on racist motivations. As described above, one reason for the rapid spread of the HIV virus among Africans is likely to be the far higher incidence of other sexually-transmitted diseases, which itself has not been satisfactorily explained since very little research has been devoted to understanding it. African AIDS patients may also have more commonly been exposed to HIV from other sources than sex: unsterile injections and incisions, and blood transfusions. So the role played by sexual transmission — and by the rate of partner change: "promiscuity" — is extremely difficult to quantify.

Statisticians studying AIDS epidemics in Western Europe and North America calculate that the doubling time — the time it takes for the number of reported AIDS cases to double — was about 11 months in 1987. Two or three years earlier, around 1984-5, the doubling time was about six months.[33] The difference between the two figures probably reflects the fact that the earlier reported AIDS cases were among the most sexually active section of the homosexual community. Since the rate of sexual partner change is one of the most important variables in the equations used to calculate the growth curve of an AIDS epidemic, the longer doubling time shows that the frequency of partner change in the remaining homosexual community is now much lower than that of two or more years ago.[34]

The limited statistics available from some Central African capital cities show that the doubling time of AIDS epidemics there was by 1985-6 probably eight or nine months.[35] This suggests that the rate of sexual partner change, among people living in Central African cities, may, on average, be considerably less than that which fuelled the spread of HIV in San Francisco and New York, before education programmes or other factors slowed the rate of transmission.

What such overall statistics obscure, however, is that any country or region's AIDS epidemic really looks like not one but several epidemics, each spreading like ripples in a pond. Each set of ripples represents the way in which the virus spreads from a point of entry into a particular sub-group of the population. In every country, rates of partner change will vary greatly between sub-groups. People in some groups, like truck-drivers, travelling businessmen, prostitutes and the more sexually active North American homosexuals, will have "fast-track" sexual lifestyles featuring large number of partners, while the overall average rate of partner change will be much lower.

For example, a 10-fold increase in HIV-positivity among tested groups of pregnant women in Kinshasa, Zaire, was recorded during the decade 1970-80.[36] During the same period, some AIDS researchers believe, a 500-fold increase in HIV-positivity probably occurred among Western homosexual males.[37] These data suggest that the African mothers had a sexual lifestyle more conservative by far than the Western homosexuals. Additional comparisons appear in Figure 6.4.

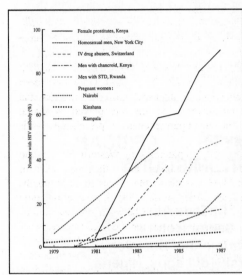

Figure 6.4: The Rise of HIV seroprevalence in various groups ["Cohort and cross-section studies of HIV seroprevalence" from P. Piot et al, *Science*, 5 February 1988, vol 239, p 75].

Such statistics may give an insight into the sex lives of particular sub-groups. But what do they tell us about the sexual behaviour of whole societies, whether our own or others? In reality, not very much. Sexual behaviour is so varied that the only way to describe it acurately is to ask people about their sex lives and collect the resulting information. Such research is seldom done because it is time-consuming, expensive and frequently embarrassing for the respondents. Until it is done, our ideas about our own and others' sexual behaviour will continue to be based more on impressions, images and prejudices than on facts.

AFRICAN "PROMISCUITY" IN PERSPECTIVE

Dr Tade Aina, a sociologist at the University of Lagos, Nigeria, thinks that Africans should not be unduly defensive about Western media coverage of AIDS which focuses on promiscuity. "We should not deny that promiscuity exists in many of our cities as it does in cities elsewhere", he says. "The term promiscuity is a relative one which can mean different things in different times and places. To understand the problem of AIDS we need to gain a perspective on why this promiscuity is happening: what are the forces which, at this particular point in time, lead many young urban Africans to take a large number of sexual partners?"

In the article below Dr Aina sketches the sociological background against which sexual behaviour in African cities has developed. He pays attention to the role played by colonial institutions, particularly those forcing husbands and wives to live apart, in fostering contemporary commercialised prostitution, and to the impact which the Western "sexual revolution" of the 1960s and 70s has had on African youth. He focuses particularly on polygamy: the practice of having more than one wife or husband at a time.

THE MYTH OF AFRICAN PROMISCUITY

BY
Dr Tade Aina
Senior lecturer
Department of Sociology
University of Lagos, Nigeria,

Many phenomena have led outsiders to consider Africans as promiscuous; polygamy is one of them. In pre-colonial times the men who had more than one wife were the elders, distinguished warriors, priests and successful traders who could pay the bride price demanded or were worthy of the dowry to be received. Marriage was about alliances between families and therefore involved kinship connections in which the emphasis was not on mutual sexual attraction or physical bonds. Not all men could marry more than one wife, and some had no wives at all.

Other forms of marriage in Africa which appear unusual to outsiders, including the inheritance of a dead sister's or dead brother's spouse, often have very limited physical sexual basis and are based on access to property and rights of inheritance. They reflect the unequal position of women in these societies, who may have no legal rights of existence except through a husband and who must be seen as wives even if this does not involve the obligations of physical sex.

The prevalence of semi-nudity may suggest to Europeans sexual availability but it is more a case of comfort and convenience. Relaxed attitudes to the body are often accompanied by rigid rules about sexual interaction and eligibility for marriage. Fertility dances and dances that celebrate puberty, maidenhood and bridal status indeed express appreciation of the human body, but are no more suggestive in the sexual sense than some European folk-dances, ice-skating and ballet in which women throw up their legs in front of a paying audience.

Although there is tremendous diversity in cultural groupings in Africa, throughout the continent sexual life is surrounded by rites and rules that tie up with age and entry into adult life. These include female and male circumcision, child marriage, early betrothal, the control of age-grades over such sources of brideprice and dowry as cattle, the various tests of manhood which certain groups subject their young men to before they can take wives, and the importance, in fact near fetishism, of virginity among some groups. All of these limit the access or the rights of young men to sexual interaction with young girls, while other sanctions against the breaching of sexual protocols range from fines to ostracism and in certain cases corporal punishment and homicide. Along with the more mundane sanctions are mystical ones such as oath-taking, putting spells and curses on culprits and invoking the displeasure of ancestral spirits.

Various arrangements in some pre-colonial urban centres and among certain warrior communities came very close to prostitution, but the sale of sex for money only came with monetisation and, of course, the European presence. Colonial policies needed cheap African labour for such activities as mining and construction, while denying the workers permission to bring their families to live with them, so they would not have any claims for urban land.

Africans could only live in towns if they had employment and could show proof of it, a system of control of population movement of which current South African pass laws are only a perfection. With men housed in barrack-like accommodation for periods of up to a year, the authorities encouraged or turned a blind eye to the growth and spread of brothels. Prostitution also spread wherever there were centres of trade and administration, and sometimes led to the emergence of ethnic specialisation as women from one area were recruited into brothels in cities elsewhere. In this sense prostitutes were also a type of migrant labour.

Another effect of colonial urbanisation was the breakdown of traditional rules and protocols of marriage, leading to unprecedented inter-ethnic marriages and sexual contacts. The new anonymity offered by cities made their inhabitants accessible to foreign and alien contacts both for transient sexual and more lasting relationships. The pluralism of urban life leaves individuals without the strict regulation of sex and marriage which the ethnic culture once provided, with no formal rules applicable to liaisons between partners from different ethnic groups or between Africans and outsiders.

Westernisation has brought with it not only new airports, roads and institutions but also the adoption of Western lifestyles, tastes and fashions. Modern young Africans look to Europe and North America for fashion, music and dance. They accept Levi jeans along with Coca-Cola, rock music, heroin and free sex.

In the immediate post-independence affluence of countries such as Nigeria or Kenya, the urban young have both the money and the leisure to enjoy a lifestyle which includes extensive and varied sexual activities. Their prey might be called the "new poor": the massive pool of young women living in the most deprived conditions in shanty towns and slums across Africa, who are available for the promise of a meal, new clothes, or a few pounds. The same poor, whether as prostitutes or as clerks and petty officials pre-disposed to taking bribes, are vulnerable to the hard currency offered by foreign visitors. Their sexual availability is born out of real material needs and reinforced by imported norms that advocate free sex.

This is contemporary sexual life in many African cities and towns, were many people take their cue from London, Paris, New York and the rest of the 'civilised' world. Their attitudes may reinforce a myth of African promiscuity, but the worldwide breakdown in sexual restraints and control is not a specifically African problem.

THE ROLE OF PROSTITUTION

Prostitution is an important factor in the spread of all STDs, both from one country to another, and within a country.[38] Prostitutes from neighbouring countries are thought by some researchers, for example, to have brought HIV to Kenya.[39] Prostitutes are given as the source of infection by 80% of male STD patients in Africa and Asia, as against

20% in North America and Europe.[40] Of course, the sexual partners of prostitutes are equally important in the spread of infection — a fact too often underemphasised in discussions of prostitution.

As female STD patients are on average 10 or more years younger than males, these statistics highlight the presence of a class of young, otherwise unemployed and often geographically mobile young women in African and Asian cities.

Traders, smugglers, soldiers, businessmen, refugees and other travellers also appear to have played an important role in the dissemination of HIV throughout Central and East Africa. Their activities during military conflicts, as in southwest Uganda and northwest Tanzania during Uganda's civil war, are probably consistent with the later appearance of AIDS in the region.

A high degree of mobility of large groups of people is a feature of African life which supports the argument that STDs, AIDS and a degree of promiscuity are consequent on extensive population movements into and between cities. Rates of STDs, HIV infection and AIDS are highest in cities, which serve as a melting pot for diverse peoples, cultures and beliefs. Some rural areas, in contrast, seem to exhibit both stable patterns of behaviour *and* rates of HIV.[41]

Africans and others in the Third World, whose main picture of social life in the West probably comes from films and TV soap operas, get an impression of societies which are highly promiscuous. And Western images of African sexual behaviour are arguably even more unreliable. Unfortunately, there is surprisingly little hard statistical information on the rate of sexual partner change in Western societies, and even less on communities in the Third World.

Scientific studies of the dynamics of AIDS epidemics in Africa are urgently needed, and until they are performed conclusions about the precise role and degree of "promiscuity" involved in AIDS in Africa are premature.[42]

THE POSSIBLE ROLE OF GENES

The rapid spread of heterosexually-transmitted AIDS among black people in Africa and the United States, and the fact that no significant epidemics of AIDS have yet surfaced in Asia, have led some medical researchers to consider whether different ethnic groups vary in the ease with which they can become infected with the HIV virus, or in the speed at which they develop and die from AIDS once infected.

Many Africans and US blacks feel that even to entertain this question betrays racist attitudes. There would indeed be considerable difficulty, if a genetic predisposition to AIDS did exist, in distinguishing it from non-genetic factors such as greater poverty, malnutrition and ill-health among some ethnic communities; from poorer access to medical facilities; and from the greater extent to which some ethnic groups are affected by family-breakdown, casual sex, prostitution and illegal drug use.

There *are* examples of inherited genetic factors which predispose some ethnic groups to certain diseases, for example sickle-cell anaemia. In tropical Africa 10-30% of the population carries the sickle-cell gene, without which this form of anaemia is impossible. The disease accounts for 80,000 infant deaths per year. Found much less frequently in the Middle East and India, the gene is unusual among white people, except in restricted parts of Italy and Greece.[43]

Is it likely that genetic factors contribute to the rapid spread of AIDS among black people, both in the United States and in Africa?

Since genetically-linked diseases do exist, this possibility must be allowed, though its importance should not be exaggerated. Research into the supposed genetic bases for AIDS could lead to better treatments or even a cure. But preventing more infection by HIV is something we already know how to do: minimising or eliminating risky behaviours through education remains the ultimate weapon against AIDS, whatever racial or sexual group is involved.

Certainly, AIDS has a different pattern of symptoms in Africa than in Europe and North America. AIDS patients in Europe more often suffer from a particular type of pneumonia, while those in Africa show more diarrhoea and gastrointestinal illness; this is why AIDS in East Africa is known as "slim disease", from the wasting away of the body caused by persistent diarrhoea. And in the United States it appears that homosexual AIDS patients are more likely to suffer from the skin cancer called Kaposi's sarcoma than are heterosexuals.

These differences, though, are almost certainly not genetic but immunological. AIDS causes a breakdown of the body's immune system, weakening and eventually destroying its defences against other "opportunistic" infections. Which infections then invade the body depends on the disease environment which the patient inhabits, on disease organisms the patient has been exposed to previously, and on the strength of the patient's immune system. These in turn are related to development, nutrition and poverty.

For example, a team of US and Zairean researchers have reported that when US adults are compared with Africans, the latter had more stimulated immune systems. "Africans", the authors said, "are more frequently exposed, due to hygienic conditions and other factors, to a wide variety of viruses [and] microbial agents which could result in ... rendering the host more susceptible to HIV infection." These findings, they conclude, "may help to explain the rapid spread of HIV infection among the general heterosexual population of tropical developing countries."[44] Clearly, the general health level and disease environment varies among different countries and ethnic communities, so AIDS will show itself in different ways.

But are there any *inherited* factors which affect AIDS? Can genes be shown to operate in such a way as to create either a resistance or a predisposition to AIDS in some people? Two groups of researchers, one in Britain and the other in Trinidad, have presented data which they believed gave a qualified "yes". In neither case have their findings been confirmed by other researchers. Several groups have tried, and failed, to reproduce the British data.

GENES: HARD EVIDENCE LACKING

In May 1987, some British scientists reported that a gene called *Gc* was more common among AIDS patients than among the population as a whole. The researchers studied homosexual men who had not contracted the HIV virus despite having regular, unprotected anal sex with infected partners; none of them had a variant of this gene called *Gc- 1f-1f*, and a quarter of them had *Gc 2-2* .

But among AIDS patients, 30% had *Gc 1f-1f*, while none of them had *Gc 2-2*. And among a control group of healthy heterosexuals, fewer than 1% had *Gc 1f-1f*.

So it looked as if *Gc 2-2* protected against infection by HIV, while *Gc 1f-1f* made people liable to infection. Moreover, *Gc 1f- 1f* also appeared to be linked to a greater likelihood of progress to AIDS after infection.[45]

The *Gc* gene is known to work in the body to make a protein which helps transport vitamin D into the cells. One theory is that the presence of this protein makes it easier for the HIV virus to get into human cells.

The British researchers also found that people with black or yellowish skin have higher frequencies of the *Gc 1f-1f* gene than white populations.[45] *Gc 1f-1f* is also commoner among some African peoples than among whites, and among US blacks than among US whites.

Could the greater extent of *Gc 1f-1f* among blacks explain the more rapid heterosexual spread of HIV in Central Africa and among US blacks? An intriguing possibility, although this hypothesis has yet to find confirmation among any of the other scientific groups that have tested it.

Data arguing for a genetic link to AIDS have also been published by Caribbean researchers. In Trinidad, 41% of the people are of African descent, 41% are ethnically Indian, and 16% are of mixed race, together with 1% ethnic Chinese and 1% ethnic Europeans.

At present, more than 90% of Trinidad's AIDS cases have been diagnosed in people (mainly homosexual or bisexual men and their partners) of African or mixed African origin. People of Indian origin, who comprise an identical fraction of the country's total population, provide less than 5% of AIDS cases. Moreover, the rate of HIV-positivity in the two groups (in both of which the degree of homosexual and bisexual behaviour was similar, according to researchers) were much closer: of 106 healthy homosexual men tested in 1983, 40% of those of African descent, and 37.5% of those of Indian descent were HIV carriers. The researchers thought it looked as if people of African and Indian descent might be equally likely to pick up the virus, and that those who were ethnically African might be more likely to develop AIDS.

Trinidad scientists began to suspect that people of African descent might have some genetic or other factors predisposing them to AIDS, and that these factors might also account for the relatively low frequency of AIDS among Indo-Trinidadian HIV-positives.[47] On the other hand, they could not rule out the possibility that the apparent differences between ethnic groups merely reflected different times of entry of the virus into the different groups. Until this is done the results remain unconvincing.

The two "genetic" scientific hypotheses for AIDS published so far have been discussed here in some detail to illustrate the complexities of data and argument which surround the issue. If susceptibility to AIDS turns out to be influenced by genetic make-up, it is highly unlikely that there will be a genetic "switch" which works in an on-off fashion, making some individuals or ethnic groups vulnerable to AIDS and others immune. The role of genes is likely to be much more complex, with various genes interacting to modify the individual's vulnerability to infection by the AIDS virus, to modify the likelihood and speed of developing fatal AIDS, or to vary the range of symptoms shown. Medical scientists have hardly begun to understand the multiple factors which may be involved.

GENES AND RACISM

The controversial nature of suggestions about the possibility of ethnic susceptibility to AIDS is illustrated by the response which the British team drew from an Ghanaian physician, who claimed they had "broadcast to the world ... the impression that there was something wrong with Central Africans, hence their plight vis-a-vis AIDS".[48]

One member of the British group, immunologist Dr Anthony Pinching, commented on this charge to Panos. "We reported our results and drew attention to their possible implications for the AIDS epidemic in Central Africa. It would have been irresponsible of us not to have drawn attention to this possibility, which was consistent with known facts and may help to explain the tragic situation which has arisen in the region."[49]

In the United States a number of respected AIDS researchers have taken an opposite view. "In discussing the issue of AIDS among minorities, it is important to stress that so far there is no evidence that race *per se* is a biological risk factor for vulnerability to AIDS. That is, in spite of the fact that greatly disproportionate numbers of blacks and Hispanics have developed AIDS, we have no reason to believe that there is any genetic reason why HIV is more likely to survive in, thrive in, or lead to disease in, blacks or Hispanics rather than non-Hispanic whites."[50]

Both the British and the Trinidadian research teams have stressed that they are not suggesting that genes are the only factors determining the course of the AIDS epidemic. To define the influence — if any — of genetic factors will involve much more research. And given the racial sensitivity of the subject, it will also involve much more heated debate.

As with some of the other racial and ethnic aspects of AIDS covered in this book, it might be helpful in future to separate these discussions from concepts of blame. And the focus on the biology of different races should not make us forget that, with AIDS more than almost any other epidemic, it is what people think, believe and do which increases the risk of infection, far more than who they are and which group they belong to.

CHAPTER SEVEN

BLAME AND COUNTER-BLAME

So far, this book has discussed some of the aspects of AIDS which have had racial and ethnic implications, and which have triggered off reactions of blame and counter-blame: the various theories on the origins of AIDS, the question of promiscuity, and the possibility that some ethnic groups are especially vulnerable to the AIDS virus.

This chapter documents African and other Third World criticisms of international research and media coverage on AIDS.

It is clear that blaming others has been a depressingly consistent theme in the debate on AIDS: in scientific circles, in the media, among politicians, and among the general public in both North and South. It is not the purpose of this book to make detailed judgments about epidemics of blame (largely in the North), or about the resentment and counter-blame (largely in the South) which they have provoked.

Some Western comments on AIDS have undoubtedly been deliberately racist, and some research and media coverage has probably been racially biased, whether consciously or unconsciously. Some Third World and ethnic minority reactions have been eminently justified; others have probably been overly defensive, seeing criticism and prejudice where none was intended, or denouncing foreign comments as racist in order to divert attention from AIDS at home. Readers must draw their own conclusions.

But blaming others, no matter how psychologically comforting it may be, offers no safety from the AIDS virus. Instead, such prejudice fouls the very channels of communication which are essential to the task of public education for AIDS prevention. Already, blame and counter-blame have seriously interfered with scientific research, and with mobilising governments and public to fight against AIDS, in Africa and other places.

RESENTMENT FROM HAITI

The earliest charges that racism was influencing the way that Western scientists and media discussed AIDS came, not from Africa, but from Haiti. The 1982 statement by the US Centers for Disease Control, that

Haitians might be a separate risk group for AIDS was quickly translated into news stories linking Haitians with the mystery homosexual disease, leading to victimisation of Haitian immigrants in the United States, and a collapse of Haiti's tourist industry.

Haitian schoolchildren were beaten up, and families were evicted from their homes, reported a New York city commission. The shaky Haitian economy could not withstand the stigma of AIDS. Says Dr Marie-Marcelle Deschamps, a Haitian physician prominent in her country's fight against the disease: "I think AIDS is what did it in Haiti. It became the last straw, and I know a lot of people who picked up and left because of it".[1]

As described in Chapter Four, Haitian doctors resented the categorisation of their nation as a high-risk group for AIDS along with homosexuals and drug addicts. They saw it as a misinterpretation of epidemiological data. The problem was compounded by the unfamiliarity of non-Haitian US researchers with Haitian attitudes toward homosexuality and illegal drug use, combined with an inability to speak French or Haitian Creole when interviewing patients. The Haitian physicians' arguments eventually won out, and in 1985 the CDC withdrew its classification of Haitians as a risk group — but not soon enough to undo the damage done to Haitians both in the United States and in Haiti.

It is widely believed among Africans that Western research into the possibility that AIDS originated in Africa has also been at least partially based on slipshod science, motivated by a wish to prove that AIDS started somewhere other than in the United States.

AFRICAN SUSPICIONS OF WESTERN RESEARCH

One of the first widely-publicised origins theories was that AIDS was an old African disease, and, as described in Chapter Three, the earliest examination of old blood samples led to the false conclusion that HIV had been endemic in Africa for decades. Physicians living and working in Africa found the suggestion that AIDS might have been present among their patients for years, unnoticed and undiagnosed, both improbable and insulting. When methods for testing blood for HIV antibodies improved, the early blood tests were discredited and it was accepted that AIDS was as new to Africa as it was to the United States and Europe.

One of the second most popular origins theories was that HIV had evolved from a parent virus, discovered in wild African green monkeys, passed to African people and thence to the rest of the world. Again, African scientists found the theory improbable, a view which seemed not unreasonable after the well-publicised evidence for the existence of an African green monkey virus turned out to be a case of mistaken identity on the part of US researchers.

It is hardly surprising that many Africans, and other people from the Third World, now regard with greatest scepticism any theories that AIDS originated in Africa. African journalists and commentators have found two general grounds for suspicion. The first is that the theories for the African origin of AIDS have often been accompanied by what they regard as ill-informed and racist speculation. The second ground is that much of the origins research seems to have been directed almost exclusively at Africa, and away from major AIDS epidemics in the United States and Europe.

Said Ghana's official newspaper, the *Ghanaian Times*, in 1987 about the green monkey theory: "This is a shameful, vulgar and foolish attempt by white supremacists to push this latest white man's burden onto the doors of the black man".[2]

Africans did not merely object to what they saw as insufficient rigour in the African origins theory, and the apparent lack of interest among Western researchers in seeking an origin of AIDS outside Africa. They resented even more what they saw as offensive assumptions about African culture and sexual behaviour: the continuing stream of conjecture which was widely reported in the international media. Previously, they commented, the black nation of Haiti had been blamed as the source of AIDS, when US researchers suggested that African swine fever passed from Haitian pigs to humans via eating pork or via unnatural sexual practices. Now it was Africa's turn.

Many Africans are scornful of outside speculation on African cultural and sexual practices which might have spread the AIDS virus from monkeys to humans. The possibility that anal intercourse, or intercourse with monkeys, or ritual inoculation of the erogenous zones of men and women with monkey blood, could have passed the virus from animal to human hosts was seen in Europe and the United States as legitimate speculation. In Africa it was seen as offensive and racist.

Far-fetched as such speculations may be, says Kenyan journalist Wanume Kibedi, "many in the end gain the ring of truth simply because they are repeated often enough".[3]

"What seems to have happened", says a physician (who did not wish to be named) from one of the worst AIDS-affected Central African countries, "is that some of the Western press and researchers have used the seropositivity data we supplied, but instead of putting HIV under the microscope they have put our society, our customs, even our love life under the lens. Do you find it surprising that some of us resent this? Whatever goes wrong, whether it is famine, war, politics, or anything else, it is always because we Africans are more incompetent, corrupt, bloodthirsty or immoral than other people. We just get tired of it — we give you information and so often you seem to turn it against us."[4]

Another reason for the resentment of many African scientists about AIDS research is the disparity of access between Africa and the West in access to the scientific and international media, and the difficulty African scientists have getting international funding for their work.

Uganda, by illustration, one of the African countries both most affected by AIDS and most actively organising to combat it, was pledged US$6.8 million by bilateral donors for the first year of its five-year AIDS programme, whith international aid organisations promising it US$20 million in June 1987.[5] In comparison just one American university, Johns Hopkins in Baltimore, Maryland, had an AIDS research budget for 1987 alone of US$42 million, with an additional US$40 million for grants to other organisations and researchers.

And while the United States, Europe and the Warsaw Pact countries spend US$500-600 per capita on health services, sub-Saharan Africa on average can afford only US$8. In West Europe there is one doctor for every 470 patients; Zambia has one per 7,000 patients, and Uganda one per 21,000. While the United States has 123 medical schools and the United Kingdom has 31, Kenya, Uganda, Zaire and Zambia have only one each. The whole African continent has only 45 bio-medical journals, but 420 are published in the UK alone.[6]

There is undoubtedly an enormous gap in scientific resources between developing African countries and the developed nations that have been setting the international AIDS research agenda. This disparity makes it difficult for African scientific views to reach an international audience. But the favourite target of Africa criticism has been the Western media.

MEDIA BLITZ HITS AFRICA

After Haitians in the United States had been defined as a special risk group for AIDS, Dr Jean William Pape, a leading Haitian AIDS researcher, soon became disenchanted with the Western press, claiming that it ignored "the efforts of the Haitian people to fight, with almost no resources, the most devastating disease of this century". He told Panos: "I have given over 60 interviews to American and other reporters about AIDS in Haiti". It is very time-consuming and exhausting, and takes energy I would like to put into my work. Of all those interviews there are only one or two that recorded what I said, and the context in which I said it, accurately. The others often painted a picture of AIDS in Haiti that was unrecognisable to me."[7]

Many Africans have come to share this sentiment. Uganda was the first, and for some time one of the very few, African countries to confront its AIDS epidemic in the full glare of international media attention. This open policy — President Museveni scornfully dismissed as "backwardness" the refusal of some other African countries to be equally frank — contributed greatly to the world's awareness of the problem of AIDS in Africa, and Uganda received material and technical support from many donors as a result.

But the policy meant that during 1986-87 reporters flocked to the country to capture the story of AIDS in print and on film. Overworked health ministry officials gave hundreds of interviews and briefings; staff at medical centres answered the same questions again and again; patients in hospitals found their personal details turning up in international newspapers; prostitutes and truck drivers became overnight authorities on the sexual habits of the nation; a foreign film crew, desperate for footage of AIDS victims, burst without permission into a mission hospital outside Kampala and began filming the patients without permission. So many international stories appeared about Uganda's "slim disease" that the authorities began to wonder whether Uganda could ever be mentioned without conjuring up the image of a country devastated by AIDS.

"You would get the feeling", says Dr David Serwadda, senior house officer at Makerere University hospital in Kampala, "that these people had a view of the situation which they only wanted to confirm. Reporters seldom seemed to get it right, and did a lot of damage as a result. ... I've been misquoted by so many big newspapers I won't bother to give the whole list. Sometimes local newspapers are just as bad. I've stopped talking to the press much about AIDS now."[8]

A Scots surgeon who practised in Uganda for 18 years until 1987 agrees that misquotation and misunderstanding with the press were a problem. But there was another side to the story, says Dr Wilson Carswell, who is currently working on AIDS research and is based in the United States. "It was important to speak to the press because at least they were listening when no-one else was. Lots of reporters got it wrong but many reported very well and responsibly." Carswell's departure from Uganda resulted partially from his outspokenness on AIDS when "the powers that be didn't want to hear about it". He believes that the media, as an extremely important channel of communication, must have access to accurate and reliable information about AIDS. "If you refuse to tell the press what's going on", he says, "you can't really be surprised if they get it wrong because they've had to turn to less reliable sources. It's a vicious circle which can only be broken by openness and respect for truth on both sides."[9]

THE AFRICAN REACTION

Condemnation of Western reporting on AIDS has appeared throughout the African press, with articles which discuss promiscuity drawing particularly acid responses. An October 1986 London *Times* headline "Nightmare of a raddled city: promiscuity and lack of medical resources have made Kinshasa the AIDS capital of the world" was one such story.[10] The article went on to comment that "sexual promiscuity is rife in Kinshasa, as in most central African towns and cities ... few observers expect much lasting change in sexual behaviour".[11]

African journalists hit back. Western reporting on AIDS was a "campaign of systematic denigration against black Africa" said the Cameroon newspaper *La Gazette* in July 1987;[12] it "deliberately encourages racism and reinforces racist ideologies", said the Ivory Coast newspaper, *Fraternité-Matin* in August 1987.[13] *New Vision* in Uganda referred to "Western escapism and racist hangups"[14]

The idea that AIDS had started in Africa was repeatedly denounced: it was reminiscent of a "colonial mentality which capitalises on our weakness and underdevelopment to attribute everything that is bad and negative to the so-called dark continent", said Lt-Col Abdul Mumini Aminu, governor of the Nigerian state of Borno.[15] Just as Africans saw the West as blaming AIDS on Africa, some of them now blamed it back on the West. "Today pornography in Western cities coveys a lurid tale of a society which has gone berserk in its sexual habits [with] negative consequences for world public health", wrote a correspondent in the Nigerian magazine *African Concord* in January 1987. Westerners had brought AIDS to Africa with their "weird sexual propositions[16] — a view echoed by *La Gazette* in July 1987, which referred to Westerners coming to Africa with their "sexual perversions".[17] "Many of the venereal diseases now found in Kenya", said an editorial in the Kenyan *Standard,* "were brought into the country by the same foreigners who are now waging a smear campaign against us."[18]

As assertion was piled on counter-assertion, the acrimonious debate acquired the rhetoric of North-South confrontation. "The subject of AIDS in Africa", a Nigerian journalist interjected, at a meeting on family planning in Swaziland in August 1977, "is part of an American agenda-setting in the Third World, with Washington hatching scandals to discredit Third World countries."[19]

THE RACIST FRINGE

Unsurprisingly, AIDS has been exploited by a few aggressively racist white groups in some Western countries, notably the US and France. In the opinion of most whites in these countries, these are the views of an insignificant minority. Some black organisations have, however, taken them more seriously, fearing a swell of open racism which blames black people for spreading AIDS.

The *Thunderbolt,* a broadsheet published by a small US "white power" group called the National States Rights Party, argued in 1987 that AIDS comes from Africa, and is endangering the white race through the irresponsibility of black bisexual men in the United States. Blacks are "genetically prone to AIDS"; black men are then infecting white women, who are "victims of race-mixing."[20]

Another obscure US fringe group, the Christian Defense League, wrote in August 1987 that "whites who have debased themselves by having sex with the colored carriers risk becoming gravely ill. ... White homosexuals could have started their race's exposure to AIDS by seeking out colored sexual partners. ... Regardless, whites in the beginning got AIDS from colored."[21] The Ku Klux Klan has also spoken about AIDS, calling for "a worldwide Christian movement to fight the tyranny of the black race". Homosexuals who "spread AIDS" should be charged with murder. "Innocent people have nothing to fear," the Klan said, "but we do stand against blacks, communists and homosexuals."[22]

The French political party, the Front National, which believes that France is being "swamped" by African immigrants, has found AIDS a useful extra argument. In July 1987, a magazine published from party-linked offices in Nice explained that AIDS was started in Africa by a black man who sodomised a monkey — a supposedly essential fact that, the article said, was being deliberately suppressed by the French health authorities.[23] While the political influence of the US racist groups quoted above is comparatively small, the Front National gained over 14% of the vote in the April 1988 French presidential election.

Though such ideas may be accepted by very few whites, they are one reason for the strong counter-views expressed by some blacks in Europe and the United States. "Africans are studied by researchers as if they are animals in a zoo ... Black people are commonly accused of bringing venereal diseases into Western countries", wrote the London-based Black Health Workers and Patients Group in March 1987 in "The AIDS Frame-up".[24] And a black US psychiatrist, Dr Frances Welsing, told a November 1987 conference on AIDS and racism held in London that HIV had been invented by whites to destroy blacks, to whom they are genetically inferior and whom they subconsciously resent for their colour.[25]

Black commentators on AIDS[26] still refer, as an example of unethical and racially-biased scientific research, to the Tuskegee experiment exposed by the *New York Times* in July 1972. In 1932 the US public health service started a study which continued for over 40 years to examine the effects of the disease. Between 28 and 100 of the men are thought to have died as a direct result of this lack of treatment, which continued after the discovery of penicillin. One analysis of the Tuskegee experiment has documented how the white doctors who initiated it subscribed to notions that blacks were racially inferior to whites, were inherently susceptible to disease, had little control over their passions, and were a "notoriously syphilis-soaked race".[27]

As long ago as 1981, US black activist and academic Angela Davis argued that racial bias pervaded US medicine particularly when sex was involved: "The domestic population policy of the US Government has an undeniably racist edge. Native American, Chicana, Puerto Rican and Black women continue to be sterilised in disproportionate numbers ... 43% of the women sterilised through federally subsidised programmes were black."[28]

In the United States, the advocacy of abortion and sterilisation for women of child-bearing age who are HIV-positive could cause considerable concern in the future; as described in Chapter Two, a high proportion of US HIV-positive women are black or hispanic. Scholars looking at the ethical implications of AIDS have already warned that there could be increasing pressures for such measures. Ronald Bayer of the Hastings Center, an institute specialising in ethics in biology and medicine, told *Time* magazine in July 1987: "I am certain there will be a lot of calls for the sterilisation of infected women".[29]

In cities such as New York, where intravenous drug use has led to the birth of nearly 200 black and hispanic babies with AIDS, such calls could be seen as racially motivated. Discussing the prospect of abortion and sterilisation for HIV-positive ethnic minority women, Dr Stephen Thomas of the health education department of the University of Maryland said in November 1987: "If policymakers do not at the same time develop a sensitive strategy to do something for these people, the perception in those communities could well be that they are experiencing a form of genocide".[30]

The fact that racist groups try to exploit AIDS underlines the need for great care and sensitivity when governments and others discuss and respond to it.

THE COST OF COUNTER-BLAME

The danger with the intense reaction which Western discussion of AIDS has sometimes provoked in Africa is that it diverts attention from effective action against the epidemic. Comments Dr S. I. Okware, head of Uganda's national AIDS prevention committee: "There is a snake in the house. Do you just sit and ask where the snake came from? Should we not be more concerned with what action needs to be taken now that the snake is in the house?"

The vigorous critique of international AIDS coverage in the African press has in some countries discouraged both domestic and foreign journalists from honestly reporting the issue. "This is unfortunate", says Dr Kwesi Tsiquaye, a Ghanaian virologist currently working at the London School of Hygiene and Tropical Medicine, "because it is the role of the media to alert people to the danger of AIDS. Information should not be suppressed just because some people don't like to hear it. On the other hand, we must recognise that these are matters of high sensitivity which require — but have not always received — exceptionally accurate and perceptive reporting."

An African physician who has worked in Kenya, Zambia and Uganda told Panos in October 1987 that he had observed "a gradual recognition that hiding the problem is counterproductive. The Ugandan approach, which was quite open and unrestrictive in terms of information, probably succeeded better in getting a national AIDS programme off the ground earlier".[31]

Newspapers in some African countries now openly acknowledge that AIDS was until recently something to keep quiet about. "A few years ago", said the *Times of Zambia* in August 1987, "there was an unwritten rule not to discuss the presence of AIDS in Zambia so as not to discourage tourists from coming here. It was a policy of the ministry of health not to alarm the public.[32]

The same applied in Nigeria, according to Nigerian magazine *Newswatch* in March 1987: "In the six years since the AIDS scourge spread across the world, Nigeria has tried its best to wish it away. No co-ordinated efforts were made to find out whether or not the disease was already present in Nigeria, and if so, how to contain it. Not until last year did [the health minister] first send a five-man team to Geneva to learn the basics of coping with the disease, ...the federal government is now scrambling to cover lost ground."[33]

Exasperated at what they saw as inflation of their AIDS statistics, or wanting to play down the degree of infection, some African governments have banned AIDS researchers and physicians from talking to the press. "One result of such attempts at control", said James Brooke, West African correspondent for the *New York Times,* in November 1987, "has been to force foreign reporters to rely more heavily on foreign researchers working in those countries, making it more difficult than before to convey an authentically African point of view".[34]

Ellen Hale, a medical reporter for the US Gannett News Service, convinced her editor to allow her to spend six months travelling in and writing on AIDS in the Third World. In 1987 she visited Zaire. "I kept bumping into US researchers there who were scared to death to be seen with me. They thought that if I went back and wrote a story they would be accused of leaking sensitive information."[35]

VIEWS FROM THE STREET

The epidemics of blame and counter-blame triggered off by AIDS have repeatedly stalled effective government action. They have created in many parts of Africa (as elsewhere in the world) serious misconceptions about how ordinary people should protect themselves against the disease.

Andrew, a bricklayer in Lusaka, told Zambian journalist Dave Moyo in August 1987: "It is the whites who brought this disease. Just look at the way some of them want to sleep with their fellow men and Zambian boys." He considers that whites have killed Zambian culture and that "before the white man came an African had a pure sex life. But then they brought their so-called civilisation, their big hotels where they practise their immorality."[36] And a survey of Zambian medical students found that the Western publicity about AIDS in Africa had convinced them the disease could not be serious in their country.[37]

One danger of blaming others for AIDS is that it allows people at risk to miscalculate the dangers, and undermines AIDS education campaigns. Yinka, a Nigerian prostitute based in the vice district of Lagos, told Nigerian reporters in early 1987 how AIDS had meant that African men avoided prostitutes known to have slept with the "dirty foreigners" who had brought the disease to the country. And Juliet, another prostitute operating from one of the big tourist hotels, explained how prostitutes in Lagos were resolved that their white clients should wear condoms: "Although white clients generally pay better than their African counterparts, I will never go to bed with a white man unless he wears a condom. As far as I am concerned, AIDS is a white man's disease."[38]

Cornelia, a 25-year-old Ghanaian prostitute, told reporters in August 1987: "When I tell my African customers that they should use a condom, some of them say that this AIDS scare is a lie put about by whites to prevent us Africans from having as many children as we want."[39] Kenyan hotel worker, Thomas M, sees the mass use of condoms as "a plot to keep us Kenyans down. The Europeans have failed so far to impose population control on us, so now they have invented AIDS to do the trick".[40]

WHAT JOURNALISTS THINK

Some Western journalists have been responsive to negative African reaction to their stories. Thompson Prentice covers medical issues for the London *Times* in both Africa and the United Kingdom. "I've become well aware of African reactions and criticisms", he told Panos in December 1987. "They've had an effect on me and I now try to get across the point of view that Africans and African countries have made some quite strong advances on the AIDS front, and that there are some encouraging factors. I haven't been compromised, but I've become aware that Africa has very special problems that have to be acknowledged.[41] But Prentice now believes that the subject of AIDS in Africa may be getting less touchy. At a recent AIDS conference, he was "heartened to notice the forthrightness and willingness to discuss AIDS by delegates from Africa."

A Nairobi-based Western correspondent, who wishes to remain anonymous, told Panos in December 1987: "When I wrote my piece on AIDS I wanted to get across the conspiracy of silence that allowed people to continue to be infected with the virus. [But] you know how emotional people are about AIDS. Westerners are just as subject to this as Africans. All you can do is to try to report fairly and responsibly, and not to provoke anybody into knee-jerk reactions."[42]

African journalists encounter some of the same problems. Otula Owuor, science correspondent for the Kenyan *Daily Nation*, has been highly critical of Western coverage of AIDS in Kenya, including that of the Panos Institute. He believes that coverage has been alarmist and that its effect, at least in Kenya, has been almost entirely negative. "The principal effect", he comments, "has been to arouse the suspicion that AIDS does not even exist in Kenya. [This makes] my job more difficult. If we write about AIDS, people think we are exaggerating. If we don't, they think we are covering up."[43]

Another Kenyan journalist, Hilary Ng'weno, is similarly critical of Western reporting on AIDS. "To Africans there is more than a little good old fashioned racism in much of this", he wrote in *Newsweek* in March 1987. International press coverage was "getting Africans' backs up", and time and effort was "being wasted in attempts to refute the wild claims of some reports on AIDS in Africa instead of taking the necessary countermeasures against the disease."[44]

The Western media seemed to believe that "all the world needs to do to contain AIDS is to keep Africans contained in their continent and send home those that are already living abroad", Ng'weno concluded. "What Africa needs from the rest of the world is not a never-ending siren recounting a litany of disasters about to engulf the continent. What Africa needs is concrete assistance to fight the AIDS menace."

"With AIDS we are seeing a replay of a dynamic which has occurred between the Third World, particularly Africa, and the West many times before", says Nigerian Eddie Iroh, a senior international journalist who is currently European editor of the *African Guardian* magazine. "The Western media is bigger and better funded, and possesses superior communications technology, than the Third World, and so its voice is most often heard. This dominance makes it difficult for Africans to air their point of view, and especially to combat what many see as anti-African propaganda"[45]

Panos invited Dorothy Kweyu Munyakho, a distinguished Kenyan journalist, to examine Western media coverage of AIDS in Africa, based on a selection of clippings sent to her by Panos. This is her report.

HOW THE WESTERN MEDIA GOT IT WRONG

BY
Dorothy Kweyu Munyakho
(Formerly Special Projects Editor,
Nation newspapers, Kenya)
Deputy Regional Co-ordinator
Babyfood Action Network

From studying newspaper clippings of 23 Western publications with 43 different headlines from February 1985 to July 1987, it appears that the Western press sees AIDS primarily, and perhaps uniquely, as an African problem. AIDS, they write, originated in Africa, is prevalent in Africa, is exacerbated by African cultural practices and is likely to wipe out Africa before any other continent.

Because of the stigma attached to AIDS — it was first detected among American homosexuals and intravenous drug abusers — lumping Africa as a whole with the high risk groups cannot but be seen to betray racial prejudice. This is especially so when WHO holds that "no region of the world is free from HIV infection and AIDS".

One of the means of determining bias in a publication is by reading the headline. Although the headline is supposed to reflect the content of the main story, quite a number of headlines fail to do so, and in some cases contradict it. A headline in the British magazine *New Scientist* (26 June 1986), for instance, reads: "AIDS is running rampant through Africa". The introduction to the story merely quoted WHO director-general, Halfdan Mahler, as saying there was "gross under-reporting of AIDS throughout the world". No Africa in the introduction. No

Africa in the second paragraph either. The third paragraph quoted Mahler as saying: "There is no race, no creed and no country that is immune from it". The first mention of Africa was that on the continent the disease was heterosexual, unlike in the United States, Europe and Australia, where homosexual men and drug abusers constituted the high risk group.

Although the article quoted the head of the infectious diseases clinic in Kinshasa, Zaire, as saying that AIDS was a hidden epidemic in some African cities, affecting 18 to 24% of the general population, it failed to take into account that less than 25% of the African population are urbanised. It also neglected to mention that blood-test studies of AIDS in cities such as Nairobi have centred around high risk groups, mainly prostitutes. These constitute a tiny fraction of total populations and present a misleading picture of AIDS prevalence in Africa.

Headline bias in AIDS reporting can be seen in other media. "AIDS: Africa's new agony" was the anchor headline for a series in the *Times* of London in October 1986. "A million Africans are set to die from AIDS" said another *Times* headline on 27 October 1986, though this one had a sidebar saying: "New drive to fight spread of virus". The article spoke of British efforts to fight AIDS and mentioned one, Dr Charles Farthing, who said of AIDS in Britain: "At least one hundred people become infected everyday. We are losing millions of lives." It is possible to speculate that, if the quote had been made in respect of Africa, it could have formed the headline.

"AIDS report finds virus afflicts six per cent of Africans", was a headline in the *Wall Street Journal* in July 1986, quoting a Zairean doctor. To claim that 6% of Africans carry the virus without comparing this with the prevalence for other continents, and without stating how the percentage was arrived at, is bound to arouse suspicion about the credibility of the story.

Other racially-biased headlines include "Africa in the plague years" *(Newsweek,* 1 December 1986), "Africa: a continent devastated by AIDS. Million Africans face death from AIDS" *(Financial Times,* 25 March 1987), "AIDS seen as threat to Africa's future" (*Washington Post,* 31 May 1987), and "African AIDS 'deadly threat to Britain'" (*Daily Telegraph,* 21 September 1986: quote marks part of headline). *Africa Now,* which is owned by Africans, but is published in London, also carried a headline typical of Western media in November 1986: "AIDS ravaging Africa". *

Many of the November and December 1986 news reports quoted by Dorothy Kweyu were derived from the Panos Institute's dossier "AIDS and the Third

The point to note about AIDS in Africa is that the sources of information for the Western media are the same people who are

A million Africans are set to die from Aids

By Thomson Prentice, Science Correspondent, Kinshasa, Zaire

A million people in Africa will die from acquired immune deficiency syndrome (Aids) and several million are already carriers of the lethal virus, according to a new report by world experts.

The disease is spreading rapidly and almost uncontrolled across the continent and a concerted international effort to help more than 20 African nations struck by the epidemic is urgently needed, it says.

Emergency action to try to control and prevent further ...

predominantly transmitted through heterosexual liaisons.

The incidence in some African cities, such as Kinshasa in Zaire and Kigali in Rwanda, has reached between 550 and 1,000 cases for every million adults: 10 to 20 times higher than the rate in Britain and higher than anywhere else in the world.

For every case there may be up to a hundred carriers who may develop symptoms or infect others.

Increasing numbers of children are being born with traces of the Aids infection. In one maternity hospital in

18 per cent of donated blood in Kigali is contaminated.

"It is evident that the Hum...
Viru...
lishe...
and ...
rapid...
repor...
a ma...
Afric...
contr...
prog...
scree...
imm...
prior...
Ev...
were ...
says, ...
Aids ...
pa'...

...called Slim   14

MEDICINE

Africa in the Plague Years

Several hundred thousand are dead, and perhaps 5 million more carry the AIDS virus

One hundred and fifty miles south of the Ugandan capital of Kampala lies the village of Kasensero. Five years ago, 500 Ugandans lived in this settlement not far from the Tanzanian border. They seined Nile perch from Lake Victoria and traded textiles and tea to smugglers from the south. They also traded in sex. The dusty main street of mud-brick and clapboard huts was lined with disco full of prostitutes offering cut-rate sex.

In 1982 AIDS struck Kasensero. Now there are only 150 people left in the vill...

more than 100 villagers died, and many others left. Today many of the huts are empty. Funerals are a depressingly frequent event. Nurse Josephine Naruyin opened up shop just this year in a bar dispensary, eight by eight feet. "Si came here," she says, "48 people ha' from 'slim' "—AIDS, so-called by U villagers in some afflicted areas ' emaciates its victims. "We ' maid last week. She was ' discover ... and we hope the la'

"To Africans there is more than a little good old-fashioned racism" in Western media reporting of AIDS, says Kenyan journalist Hilary Ng'weno (see page 93). Headlines such as these (left, Newsweek, 1 Dec 1986; right London Times, 27 October, 1986, were seen by many in Africa as exaggerating the impact of AIDS and as blaming its spread on Africans.

attached to African national AIDS programmes. Unless these doctors are giving different reports to the media than they are passing to WHO surveillance units in the countries they are working in, then it can be said that AIDS constitutes no greater threat to Africans than it does to Western countries. Headlines like "African AIDS 'deadly threat to Britain' ", asserted without stating just how AIDS in Britain is different from AIDS in Africa, serves only to polarise the AIDS issue along racial lines.

Some Western press reports have selectively condemned African cultural practices associated with the spread of AIDS, failing to mention other cultural practices which could help curb the spread of the virus. These reports cement African opinion that Western journalists report with an anti-African bias. An example is a story entitled "Zambian Tribal Customs Add to AIDS Epidemic" in the *International Herald Tribune* of 4/5 July 1987.

In this story, the author condemns a widely practised African custom where a widow is supposed to have sexual relations with the brother of the deceased to cleanse herself of her husband's ghost. The 39-paragraph story gave only three paragraphs to another African custom, *chisungu*, which demands that teenagers refrain from sex until they are married. Why the writer chose to amplify the negative story and wrote very little about *chisungu*, which he well pointed out was gaining ground due to the emergence of AIDS, is a clear example of racial bias in AIDS reporting.**

The Western media refuses to recognise AIDS as a global problem and insists on portraying it as the Black Man's Burden. Media hype of AIDS has not had positive results. It leads to actions such as those taken by national governments to curb free international travel in spite of WHO's concern that measures such as compulsory screening of international travellers will only divert funds and attention from more effective AIDS prevention efforts.

The world needs to be informed about all that is pertinent about AIDS. This can be done by honest, truthful, factual reporting rather than stories slanted against Africans.

The **International Herald Tribune *report appeared three months after a similar story issued by Panos Features on 10 April 1987. Commissioned by Panos from Zambian journalist Dave Moyo, this shorter 22-paragraph article devoted 14 paragraphs to the general Zambian campaign against AIDS, and 8 paragraphs to the controversial practice of* **ukupyana** *whereby a widow has sex with her dead husband's brother; the Panos story did not mention* **chisungu**. *It was printed by* **New Vision** *in Uganda, and by several other African newspapers* —Panos

---

WAS PANOS RACIST?

The Panos Institute was itself criticised for racist attitudes and assumptions by some African writers, notably for material in its dossier *AIDS and the Third World*, first published in November 1986.

The *Kenya Times* ran an editorial on the dossier entitled "AIDS: Western bias smacks of racialism". Quoting statements made by health minister Peter Nyakiamo in the Kenyan parliament, the article said that the dossier's statements on AIDS in Kenya were "inaccurate, misleading, and perhaps "loaded" against Kenyans if not Africans".[46] A Kenyan *Daily Nation* journalist, Otula Owuor, who had attended a seminar organised by Panos in London when the dossier was published, wrote an article on the Panos report in December 1986 headed "AIDS: why this biased publicity?". Owuor charged that the dossier was based on "controversial data" and "behind-the-scene European and American research speculations and calculations", and that it "zeroed in on AIDS in Africa".[47] Six months later he reasserted his view, writing that the dossier was "not only based on questionable data but also designed to spread panic, fear and even discrimination against African elites".[48]

Zambia's director of medical services, Dr E. Njelesani, disputed the dossier's figures on HIV seropositivity among tested groups in Lusaka, though he "declined to give a true picture".[49] And the British weekly magazine *New Scientist*, in an editorial entitled "A virus for hysteria", described Panos as "a new lobby group in London looking for a niche".[50] Writing in the British medical journal the *Lancet*,[51] London-based Ghanaian doctor Felix Konotey-Ahulu accused Panos, together with five British newspapers and the BBC World Service, of "misinformation and disinformation" on AIDS in Africa.

In a book published in 1987 called *AIDS, Africa and Racism,* a whole chapter is devoted to criticisms of the Panos dossier. Authors Richard and Rosalind Chirimuuta (who also examine possible racist motives in researching the origins of AIDS — see Chapter Five) charged that Panos' "highly sensationalised accounts of AIDS in Africa are based on the very hit-and-run research which they [Panos] claim to criticise. For students of racism, this is classic material." [52] The chapter concluded that "the Panos dossier overwhelmingly succeeded in its purpose. Whatever the bias and factual inaccuracies of the dossier, ever gullible and uncritical journalists relayed the message to the world that AIDS is essentially an African disease."

Whether these judgments were justified or not, majority Third World opinion seemed to go the other way. Nearly 10,000 copies have been distributed by Panos to over 44 countries; many more copies have circulated in photostat. The Senegal based non-governmental organisation ENDA collaborated with Panos in publishing a West African edition of the dossier in French in April 1987.[53] The dossier has been used by many national AIDS programmes in the Third World: in Brazil. for example, where it has been translated into Portuguese for distribution to 10,000 health workers, and in Zimbabwe where 1,000 copies were locally reprinted by Ministry of Health officials in Mashonaland West for use as training material for 2,500 community AIDS educators.

Third World press comment was generally enthusiastic. The *Sunday Times* of Zambia described it in November 1986 as "a freshly comprehensive study, the first of its kind and spectrum", which "gives straightforward but frightening facts" and "simplifies language for laymen who need to know what they should do to guard against this modern invasion".[54]

In January 1987 the *Bangkok Post* called it "an extremely comprehensive report" which "has a lot to say about how each society is reacting to this dreaded syndrome", of whom "very few, as this report starkly makes clear, are doing what is desperately necessary to turn the alarming statistics around".[55] And the *Zimbabwe Herald* said in November 1987 that "although it concentrates on developing countries, it provides a global perspective and is this respect is the first balanced, comprehensive account of a deepening crisis."[56]

The vast majority of African and other Third World responses to AIDS and the Third World have been, so far as Panos is aware, positive ones. But it is clear that publishing information on AIDS, particularly in an international context, encounters more intense scrutiny, more volatile reactions, more entrenched opinions, and more diverse perspectives than almost any other topic. Success can only be measured by the extent to which information helps people to recognise, understand, and react constructively to the global threat posed by HIV and AIDS.

CHAPTER EIGHT

WHO PAYS THE PRICE OF BLAME?

For centuries, the reflex response to plague and pestilence has been to bar strangers from the city gates. Today blood tests for antibodies to HIV replace barricades but fear of contagion and its results remain the same. Press clippings, interviews and other documentary material from every continent show that the appearance of AIDS in any community has almost inevitably been accompanied by the urge to point the finger at someone else. The varieties of AIDS blaming are as numerous — and often as ill-judged — as the prejudices which existed before them.

BLAME GOES ROUND THE WORLD

Though African countries have been constant in their criticism of the United States and Europe over AIDS, Africans have also sometimes blamed ethnic minorities in their own, or in a neighbouring country.

"During the rule of the white man we had all the medicines to cure all the diseases", said Lute, a Zambian woman in her early 40s, to a Zambian reporter in Lusaka in July 1987. "But now the Indian doctors in our hospitals are saying that this disease cannot be cured. The government has mounted the AIDS campaign to hide the inefficiency of the Indian doctors."[1]

Kenya has sometimes blamed neighbouring Uganda. A May 1987 editorial in the *Kenya Times*, for example, accused Uganda of "trying to pass the buck, and the bug, elsewhere".[2]

Uganda had the largest number of reported AIDS cases in Africa, said the *Kenya Times*, the newspaper of Kenya's ruling party, and this might be linked to the fact that Ugandans were lax in matters of sexual morality. "As our Ugandan brothers and sisters are well aware, many of the people over there who occasionally fall victim to venereal diseases usually joke about their ill-luck, saying they are suffering from a fever of sorts." The editorial urged Ugandans to pay attention to the advice contained in a pastoral letter written by Kenya's Catholic bishops, who warned that "nature has its own law of retribution".[3]

APARTHEID AND AIDS

In South Africa, AIDS is sometimes discussed as if there were two separate viruses: white HIV and black HIV. The national health authorities, who by early 1988 had reported 65 cases of AIDS in white homosexuals since 1982, have only recently documented the presence of the virus in the black community. Blood test surveys have identified HIV antibodies in over 1,000 black South Africans, and doctors in South Africa's blood transfusion service estimate that as many as 15,000 blacks and 5,000 whites could now be carrying the virus. A less alarming picture is given by the chairman of the AIDS Advisory Committee, who estimates the number of black carriers at 3,000.[4]

When information that HIV had appeared among blacks became public in July 1987, the mass-market *Sunday Star* ran the headline: "Experts fear spread of African AIDS". In contrast to the AIDS already present among whites, "African AIDS" was the "heterosexual variant of the killer disease" which had "entered South Africa from the North".[5] Migrant mine workers from African neighbouring countries had brought the virus into South Africa with them, charged the *Sunday Star*, spreading it to the black South African women with whom they had sexual relations.

"There is no doubt that an epidemic of African AIDS is coming", a University of Cape Town virologist is quoted as saying, while a blood specialist is said to have remarked that "It is inevitable that we will have cases of African AIDS".[6] The government's own AIDS advisory group of medical experts publicly dismissed suggestions that there is such a thing as "African AIDS", but the distinction between "African" and "European" AIDS was maintained in some newspapers.

A REACTION TO BLAME: DISBELIEF

The perception that blame has been cast can have negative consequences, whether or not the perception is itself accurate. A sea-change in Nigerian public opinion on AIDS — from open-mindedness to suspicion and disbelief — occurred after Western scientists focused the attention of an international AIDS conference on AIDS in Africa and the possible African origins of the AIDS virus. Nigerian science journalist Seun Ogunseitan followed these events closely. His conclusion, that Nigerians' perception of blame was a serious set-back for Nigerian AIDS information and participation in international AIDS prevention efforts, is explained in the article which follows.

NIGERIA: HOW PUBLICITY PUT THE CLOCK BACK

BY
Seun Ogunseitan
Science Correspondent
The Guardian, Lagos, Nigeria

Early in December 1985 I reported in the *Guardian* that doctors in one of Nigeria's leading medical institutions might have diagnosed the country's first AIDS cases. Some of my colleagues were displeased by my having "put Nigeria on the AIDS map".

Barely six months before I wrote that first story, Nigerians had wanted to know as much as possible about AIDS. Few of them were bothered about the origin of the disease. The population was so receptive to information then that individuals who could not find explanations for weight loss, but knew it was a symptom of AIDS, were writing to newspapers anxious to know more about the disease.

The zeal with which Nigerians sought information on AIDS probably exceeded the interest in the disease of average Americans; but the fear and paranoia common in Europe and the United States were largely absent. Nigerians saw themselves as part of a global community under common threat. Unprompted, they related AIDS to men and women of "easy virtue", and wondered about the activities of suspected bisexuals.

A single event marked the transition from this atmosphere of unselfconscious enquiry. In mid-1985 an international congress was held in Brussels under the title "Conference on African AIDS". This was a major mistake. African delegates — including Nigerians — objected publicly to the title, but the rest of the researchers present failed to respond coherently to this criticism. It was at this point that the international community of AIDS researchers lost credibility with Nigerians and other Africans. The suggestion that AIDS originated in Africa and the implication that it is a disease of blacks made ordinary citizens begin to doubt the claims of these researchers.

One immediate after-effect of the Brussels conference was the adoption of secrecy by health authorities in Africa, who would otherwise have approached AIDS as a serious health issue which should not be concealed. Whereas most Nigerians had believed that the disease was killing tens of people every week in East and Central Africa, once it was suggested that it originated in Africa, they began to doubt the truth of Western media reports on the epidemic.

Before the "origins" question became an issue, the average Nigerian would have thought twice about statistics which suggested that up to 68% of adult groups in some African communities were carrying the AIDS virus; now the figures were regarded with unveiled scepticism.

In this climate of opinion my report of the arrival of AIDS in Nigeria was interpreted as "joining *them* in the preposterous assertion that the disease originated in Africa". Many reasons were found to show why AIDS should not be reported as being present in Nigeria. Talk about the severity of the problem was alternately a "gimmick to gain more funds for research", or "all Western propaganda".

Moreover, many Nigerians suspected that "the West has finally found a good ploy to force Africans to accept the use of condoms. It claims that condoms should now be used for protection against AIDS, but its real aim is to further its long-term population control plan for Africa."

At the end of 1985 many governments, particularly in Africa, were unwilling to acknowledge the presence of AIDS or even the likelihood of its presence among their citizenry. This dangerous silence was also true in Lagos, and many Nigerians wanted to keep it that way. Nigerian press reports were erroneously suggesting that AIDS was just one more dangerous sexually transmitted disease said to be ravaging communities of homosexuals and intravenous drug users in Europe and America.

Only with reluctance did the Nigerian media carry the first reports of what is now an acknowledged AIDS epidemic in East and Central Africa. To most Nigerians in 1985, AIDS was someone else's problem. It was not their disease, was not present in Nigeria — and nobody should suggest the contrary.

In writing my story I had hoped to influence the government to adopt a more open attitude towards AIDS. But due to the charges of racism which followed the Brussels meeting the import of the story was lost on many Nigerians. With the issue of the origins of the disease festering in the public mind it was impossible to make any headway in reporting how the epidemic was spreading. Even people with symptoms of the disease met hostility because of the public link between AIDS and racism.

In the meantime, the information carried in thousands of

reports on AIDS in the international press were lost on the now-biased Nigerian public. Some Nigerian scientists were vilified by the government and, to a lesser extent, the public for "joining them in confirming the presence of AIDS in the country".

There is no doubt that the opportunity for extensive Nigerian co-operation in the international fight against AIDS in the early part of the current pandemic was lost. The damage was done when Western researchers and the media aired their opinions on the origins of AIDS too early, and without taking sufficient pains to distinguish between opinion and fact. On highly sensitive issues such as this, opinions should be stated for what they are and not granted the authority of science before incontrovertible evidence to support them can be found.

BLAME IT ON THE STUDENTS

In Europe, African students have been widely blamed for AIDS. In 1987, Belgium started to impose compulsory HIV tests for all foreign students on government grants, many of whom came from Africa, especially Zaire. Soon, a new slogan — "Black AIDS" — began to appear on metro walls.[7] "Why only Third World students?" asked Ekanga Shungu, Zairean editor of a monthly African magazine in Belgium, noting that AIDS had become such a stigma that Zaireans were now afraid to talk about it.[8]

Little has appeared in the West about attitudes to AIDS in the Soviet Union and Eastern Europe, perhaps because very few cases have so far been reported. But an African student in Moscow reported in August 1987 that while "they used to refer to us as monkeys now they point and say the word for AIDS". The same month it was reported that a group of Soviet graduate medical students had written to the Academy of Medical Sciences in Moscow, vowing that as practising doctors they would block any cure for AIDS because it was a "noble disease" which would eliminate "drug addicts, homosexuals and prostitutes".[9]

"African AIDS deadly threat to Britain " ran the headline of the front-page story of the British *Sunday Telegraph* on 21 September 1986, in a classic instance of Europeans blaming Africa for AIDS. The article claimed that an investigation into the potential risks to Britain posed by AIDS in Africa, ordered by the British foreign secretary, had resulted in "a series of alarming reports" from British embassies in Tanzania, Uganda and Zambia. British diplomats, the story said, warned that African visitors to Britain "could be a primary source of infection and should be subject to compulsory tests".

The UK Foreign Office acknowledged receiving a report, but said that no immediate action would be taken. But the *Sunday Telegraph* made its position clear: "It would be monstrous if ministers were to hold back from action lest they be accused of racial discrimination. For in this instance there is a positive duty to discriminate. In the matter of AIDS", it asserted, "Black Africa does have a uniquely bad record".[10] Within a few weeks, the United Kingdom let it be known that there were no plans to screen Zambians, after strong behind-the-scenes pressure from the UK health department and from its medical advisers. From a public health point of view, to test a few score black Zambians a year, and not to test hundreds of thousands of white US tourists who visit Britain annually, was seen by many British AIDS workers as absurd and racist.

BLAME HINDERS AIDS CAMPAIGNS

But the damage had been done. Zambia's minister of health reacted quickly to the suggestion that Zambians, notably students, should be screened for the AIDS virus on entering Britain: "We will study the situation, and we may reciprocate in the same way if Britain goes ahead. After all, AIDS is a capitalist disease which is not only common in Zambia but throughout the world".[11]

The screening apparently contemplated by the British Government was seen as a political insult in Zambia, where a number of British physicians and researchers had been working in collaboration with Zambian colleagues on AIDS-related projects. An immediate consequence was some delay in plans to screen Zambian blood supplies: while health officials were determined to do this, political support for action on AIDS was still limited, and the UK testing row undermined it.

Several other AIDS projects were disrupted as a result of the British story and reaction to it, at a moment when time was critical in Zambia's battle to contain the spread of the AIDS virus. A few months before the *Sunday Telegraph* story, a medical symposium in Lusaka had been told that 17% of healthy people coming into the city's hospital for medical check-ups were HIV-positive, and that Zambia might have 6,000 babies and infants with AIDS by 1987.[12]

On the economic side, Zambian officials were worried about the consequences on tourism of the *Sunday Telegraph*'s story, particularly since the majority of tourists were European. The year 1986 had been an all-time low for the Zambian tourist trade, with revenues down nearly 25% from 1985. Although the political instability in southern Africa and international currency fluctuations contributed to this decline, Zambian officials believe that an important factor was "negative publicity campaigns in our traditional tourist markets".[13]

The fear of bad publicity about AIDS was all the more acute because Zambia has been fighting for its economic life. Declining revenue from copper, its principal export, has initiated a downward spiral which has seen per capita income fall by two-thirds since 1980. Zambia hopes tourism will offset the loss of copper earnings, by bringing in hard currency and creating even more employment than the 30,000 plus jobs which have sprung up in the wake of foreign visitors.

Following the *Sunday Telegraph* story, British researchers received a letter from a Zambian official which read in part: "I regret to inform you that the mass media in recent weeks have raised problems which require questions to be asked as to whether collaboration should be continued with outside researchers. I am afraid that we are in a political world, and such matters, as they are reported in the British press, make it difficult to continue".[14]

Zambia is not the only country to reconsider joint AIDS endeavours due to media coverage judged to be unfavourable. African sensitivities to Western research on AIDS were increased by the tendency of Western scientists to carry out "parachute" research: dropping in to collect blood samples, data or clinical observations, and just as quickly taking off again, to write up their findings for a (Western) scientific journal. African officials would find themselves in the position of first reading about the "latest" AIDS statistics from their country in such a journal or, worse, in a sensationalised account in the international press.

Undoubtedly, political tensions over AIDS have sometimes damaged the campaign to contain the disease. But not all Western researchers drop into and out of the African countries they are studying. Very often there is no clear-cut distinction between the work of expatriate researchers and that of their African counterparts. In Kenya, Rwanda, Tanzania, Uganda, Zambia, Zaire, Senegal and other African countries, foreign and African experts have been working together on a range of AIDS research and control projects, some of several years' duration. Without this international collaboration, much of the progress on AIDS control would have been impossible.

AFRICAN STUDENTS BLAMED IN INDIA

The apparent willingness of some British diplomats to blame AIDS on Zambian students was followed six months later by a similar row in India — again about students from Africa. Indian science writer, K.S.Jayaraman, describes what happened.

STORM IN INDIA

BY
Dr K. S. Jayaraman
Science Editor
Press Trust of India, New Delhi

In February 1987 the Indian Government decided to enforce strictly the screening of all foreign students for AIDS, and began deporting those found HIV-positive. Africans, who account for 85% of the foreign student population, were incensed at what they felt to be a "racist and unscientific" policy. Their nationwide protest brought AIDS to the centre of a political controversy and India, a champion of anti-apartheid, was drawn into a diplomatic row with friendly African nations over an apparently non-political issue.

It was a chance finding of AIDS antibodies in a Tanzanian student in Madras in June 1986 that led the government to focus on foreign students, particularly Africans. Earlier that year, 22 of 130 prostitutes tested in Madras had been found HIV-positive by one of the surveillance centres being run by the Indian Council of Medical Research (ICMR). Swayed by press reports about high prevalence of AIDS in Africa, ICMR casually screened a few African students in Madras. One of them turned out to be carrying the virus.

According to an ICMR spokesman, the result scared away the rest of the African students in Madras and they refused to volunteer for the test. On the one hand, ICMR was concerned about the potential threat from African students, and on the other it was sensitive to the likely political repercussions of revealing its find. It therefore kept its discovery away from the press and recommended to the Health Ministry that foreign students be compulsorily tested for AIDS. The decision was conveyed to the Department of Education in the Ministry of Human Resources and Development, which then informed heads of all universities that all foreign students must be screened for AIDS and those found positive should be expelled.

The circular was issued on 12 August 1986, but the university authorities paid little attention to it until receiving a reminder on 23 January 1987. Foreign students were directed to nearby medical centres for the AIDS test, at which point demonstrations broke out. In Delhi, about 1,000 African students held a six-hour solidarity meeting and began a procession waving banners that said "Down with Medical Apartheid" and "We are prepared to go home rather than be humiliated", before clashing with the police. In Bombay, the 500-odd African students boycotted the medical examination. Reactions elsewhere were similar.

Fear, social ostracism and psychological trauma put the educational career of African students in jeopardy. The African Students Association alleged that the AIDS test had reached such absurd lengths that the district collector of Jabalpur ordered burning of the personal effects of an African student suspected of AIDS. This led to the local population avoiding shops and hotels patronised by Africans; there was effective segregation within and outside the university. According to Salek Osoro, a Delhi University student: "We are shunned by our erstwhile friends in the university, and in the private houses where we live. We are treated as untouchables."

African diplomats were upset by the press publicity identifying students by name and nationality, and some openly criticised

When India started testing African students for antibodies to AIDS, strong protests ensued against what was seen as racial discrimination.

the government's stand. The Ugandan high commissioner in India, Dr S. C. Chebrot, said he was unhappy at the "discriminatory test loaded against the African students." The Kenyan health minister, Mr Peter Nyakiamo, who was on a 10-day tour of India in February, told his countrymen on return that "the smear campaign was exacting a devastating psychological toll on Kenyan students." Verbal protests were made to Indian heads of mission in African countries. The AIDS tests dominated the talks between India's external affairs minister, Mr N. D. Tiwari, and the Kenyan president, Mr Daniel arap Moi, during the former's visit to Kenya, where two dailies frontpaged stories of how two Kenyan students were "kicked out" of India because of AIDS.

Off the record, an Indian Government official said the whole business was mishandled by authorities of educational institutions. "Their approach was secretive and crude and they failed to explain to students the purpose of the test." Throughout the controversy, the Indian press in general was sympathetic to the plight of the African students. Describing the government's decision as "an example of unwisdom," an editorial in the *Chandigarh Tribune* said: "The government must remove the feeling from the minds of the African students that the AIDS test is aimed at them." The *Hindustan Times* said the decision was hasty and a "panic reaction". It added that by singling out students from Africa and Asia "the government in a way is casting a slur on their sexual habits." The *Times of India* said the government action was "ill thought out, insensitive and brazenly discriminatory."

The African agitation raised an uproar in the parliament. Many opposition members wanted the AIDS test scrapped because it was harmful to India's relations with African countries. However, Mr P. V. Narasimha Rao, minister for human resources and development, said the tests would continue because "AIDS is too serious a matter to be daunted by protests." All foreign students would be tested, not just Africans. The Communist Party secretary, Mr R. C. Rajeswara Rao, said the test "is humiliating to say the least" because, in effect, "it is being enforced on Africans who constitute the majority of foreign students."

The government's determination to go ahead with the screening of foreign students collapsed when the African students announced their decision to launch fresh protests. To avoid political embarrassment, the Indian Government ceded to the Africans' demand that the AIDS test would be mandatory only for fresh students.

Although India's policy has now changed to ensure anonymity of testing and the testing of all tourists staying in the country longer than a year, many students feel there is still some bias. "Why are diplomats and diplomatic staff exempted?" asked John Mageto of Delhi University. Raid Ibrahim, a student from Kuwait, asked: "Why only foreigners? Why not Indians returning from abroad?" A Palestinian pointed out that the new policy still discriminates, because it exempts the high-risk "freak-looking tourists" coming for a short stay while "attention continues to be focused on students".

KENYA: AIDS VERSUS TOURISM

At about the same time as Kenyan diplomats were defending their students in India, another AIDS row was brewing up in Nairobi and London. On 3 February 1987 the United Kingdom's *Guardian* newspaper reported that British soldiers on exercise in Kenya had been instructed to stay out of Nairobi after 6pm because of the threat of contracting AIDS and other sexually transmitted diseases. This was said to follow an earlier decision by the UK military making the port of Mombasa, and the resort town of Malindi, off-limits for British troops.[15] Soldiers returning from Kenya were "strongly advised" to have a test for the AIDS virus on their arrival in Britain. Of those who did so, none were found to be HIV carriers, although press reports in March indicated that a number had contracted other STDs.[16]

The British troops report was embarrassing to Kenya for a number of reasons. Kenya normally plays down the yearly arrival of British troops for manoeuvres. And, like Zambia, it relies heavily on its tourist industry. With more and more nations competing for the tourist dollar, and tourists easily switching from one destination to another, the responsible Kenyan officials viewed any stories about AIDS as a threat to their expansion plans. Over 650,000 visitors injected more than US$250 million into the Kenyan economy in 1986, and the tourism ministry predicted a million tourists annually by the year 2000.

The Kenya Government was already nervous about AIDS stories. In November 1985 it had banned an issue of the *International Herald Tribune* that discussed AIDS among prostitutes in Nairobi.[17] And a 1987 international conference of air traffic controllers was almost aborted when the Austrian controllers' association became alarmed at reports that mosquitoes might be spreading the AIDS virus in Africa. The Austrian association wanted a change of venue "to another city, not located on the African continent", not wishing, they said, "to expose our families to such a danger".[18]

The conference had gone ahead, but Kenyan authorities had been shaken. When the *Guardian's* troops story appeared in February 1987, the Kenyan minister of foreign affairs said it was part of a "definite overseas smear campaign" against Kenya.[19] The health minister said there was "no scientific basis for the hysterical and alarmist media presentation", and the minister for works and housing expressing his disappointment with the "holier than thou" attitude of European countries. "The promotion of tourism in our country", wrote the Kenyan *Standard*, "is a major part of our development strategy. Many Western tourists pick Kenya not only because of the natural attractions the country has to offer, but equally because of the country's political stability and high moral standards which have earned Kenyans worldwide respect."[20]

The Kenyan minister of tourism denied rumours of widespread cancellations of hotel bookings.[21] But a magazine specialising in African affairs later said that massive cancellations had ensued,[22] and the Kenyan *Daily Nation* quoted a Kenyan travel firm as losing over US$3 million in contracts with British travel agencies after the first reports of AIDS in the country surfaced in the international press.[23]

BLAMING THE FOREIGNERS

In many countries — Panos has received reports from the Middle East, China, India, Japan, Malaysia, the Philippines, Sri Lanka, Colombia, Costa Rica, Cuba, Ecuador, Mexico, Nicaragua, Venezuela, the USSR and Eastern Europe — a common target has been the "degenerate" West.

When in early 1987 a Japanese prostitute from the city of Kobe was diagnosed as having died from AIDS, the assumption that she had been infected during sexual contact with a foreigner was reached overnight. "Her death", one Japanese newspaper concluded, "was the result of an infatuation with Europe".[24] Japanese health officials told journalists that the government was looking for ways to prevent HIV-positive foreigners entering the country, since they considered that all cases of AIDS in Japan were the result of foreign contact.

This measure quickly became confused with the desire to exclude all non-Japanese. In the red-light district of Tokyo warning signs suddenly appeared: "*Gaijin* [foreigners] off limits". There was no discouragement of Japanese customers who had recently been abroad.

In a survey of schoolteachers, Professor Bin Takeda of Chiba University turned up deep-seated fears of coming into contact with foreigners. He found that 85% of the teachers knew AIDS could not be contracted from swimming pools or from Western-style toilet seats (traditional Japanese toilets are the squat variety). But 45% still said they didn't like using swimming pools or toilets in places frequented by foreigners. "Many Japanese think foreigner equals AIDS carrier," commented Dr Masayoshi Negishi, who treats AIDS patients at Tokyo's Komagome Hospital.[25]

BLAME IT ON THE UNITED STATES

Not surprisingly, the United States has been widely blamed for AIDS. When Filipina journalist Erlinda Bolido, who works for the Press Foundation of Asia, conducted an informal poll in mid-1987 for Panos on the streets of Manila, several of the people she questioned said they believed the United States was to blame for starting the AIDS epidemic. The AIDS problem started "when some people indulged [in sex] beyond God-ordained limits," said 25-year-old secretary Tess Martelino, adding that American and other homosexuals were responsible. Nineteen-year-old Anna May Sanga knew the disease is caused by a virus. "I think it comes from a virus which was originally found in an African ape," she said. But Arsenio Alano, a retired accountant aged 73, was less sure. "I read somewhere that it originated in Africa, but I always thought that like most things good or bad, Americans invented AIDS too." Added Sanga: "people who have sexual intercourse with homosexuals, with those Americans in the military bases and with call girls" are likely to catch the disease. Erlinda Bolido reports that Americans are commonly identified as being responsible for introducing the HIV virus into the Philippines, and fear of AIDS has become an additional argument for those who demand that the bases be dismantled.[26]

In a number of countries, US military and naval personnel have been blamed for spreading AIDS. In August 1987 the Turkish magazine *Islam* carried a rumour which soon became widespread in the Middle East. US soldiers in Vietnam had contracted the AIDS virus by having sex with monkeys, the magazine claimed, and then carried it back to the United States, where they spread it to others.[27] Variants of this rumour gained currency in Latin America, claiming that a US sailor had first spread AIDS around the world. Public anxiety about AIDS in Japan in 1986 led to calls for a ban on the US fleet, while in 1987 Costa Rica turned away a US warship due for a routine visit when the US Navy could not guarantee that all the seamen were HIV-negative.[28]

"Hospitality women" in the Philippines, afraid of contracting the disease from US servicemen, continue to demand that the soldiers be tested for AIDS. The Filipina women have charged that "AIDS from US military bases poses the danger of genocide". They demanded that the Philippine Government deny entry to any US serviceman not certified AIDS-free. The possibility of HIV infection brought to the Philippines by US servicemen is, in the women's opinion, sufficient to justify the cancellation of the US-Philippines military bases agreement before its current term of effect runs out in 1991.[29] In February 1988 the Philippine Government acceded. All foreign seamen are now required to be screened for HIV-antibodies.

Some US foreign policy experts believe that "access for American ships, aircraft and other military forces to foreign bases or normal ports-of-call could become a serious security problem".[30]

The claim that the HIV virus came from a US germ warfare laboratory has been widely believed in some Central and South American countries, and as AIDS spreads rapidly in Latin America and the Caribbean, placards linking AIDS to the United States have appeared during anti-US political demonstrations. At a 1987 meeting of the Pan American Health Organization in Quito, Ecuador, participants drafted a resolution which recommended that the superpowers recognise the magnitude of the threat posed by AIDS to the security of all nations, agree to arms limitations, and should allocate the resources saved to an international AIDS prevention and control fund which emphasised the needs of developing countries.[31]

The Quito meeting also highlighted one of the important aspects of AIDS which touches on racial and ethnic divisions: that of the disparities in treatment available to people with AIDS depending on their economic, social and geographic circumstances. AZT, the only drug proven to be effective in extending the lifespan of certain categories of AIDS patients is so expensive that many US AIDS patients, especially those from impoverished backgrounds in inner city black or ethnic minority neighbourhoods, do not receive it. Outside the United States and Europe, the use of AZT has met opposition by Mexican health officials on the grounds that it is prohibitively expensive. "Why should we pay hard-earned dollars to an American company for a drug to treat a disease exported to us from the US, a country that already takes many millions from us in interest payments on our debt, to treat AIDS patients, who are unlikely to survive very long in any case?", asked a Mexican participant in the Quito conference. "It is sad, but the hard facts are that for that money we could save many more lives in other health programmes."[32]

KEEPING THE FOREIGNERS OUT

Faced with a new disease whose infectious carriers may remain outwardly healthy for years, and with medical authorities recommending politically-controversial countermeasures like sex education in schools, condoms in prisons and free one-time needles for intravenous drug users, many governments have chosen to impose blood tests on suspect groups of foreigners.

Few governments have yet taken seriously the suggestion of

compulsorily testing all their own citizens. There are two problems: practical and theoretical. The practical difficulty is that the test is relatively expensive and requires many trained technicians. The theoretical difficulty is what a government then does about people who test HIV-positive. Are they to be quarantined at government expense? Encouraged not to have sex? Issued with identifying armbands? Public health officials in most countries have spoken out strongly against any form of compulsory mass blood tests; they fear that the discrimination against carriers would set back the public education campaigns which are at present the main weapon against the epidemics.

But these problems do not apply to foreigners. They can be made to pay for the tests themselves, or simply be required to produce a certificate saying they are HIV-negative. And there is no problem about what do do with foreign HIV-positives: keep them out of the country, and let their own government sort out what to do with them.

Perhaps most importantly, screening foreigners is usually politically popular. The general wish to blame AIDS on other people is satisfied; the need for politically controversial action against the disease at home can be avoided or postponed; the government will be seen as acting resolutely. Many governments have to a greater or lesser extent given in to the epidemic of blaming others.

By March 1988, 18 countries (see Figure 8.1) were known to have decided to adopt screening for at least some groups of foreigners. The World Health Organization's advice against testing tourists has so far been generally accepted. According to WHO, screening tourists is epidemiologically ineffective (because people can be carriers of the virus but still show up HIV-negative in blood tests for up to six months after being infected), and it diverts attention from measures (such as screening blood supplies and educating the public at home) more likely to slow down the epidemics.

WHO's remit does not extend to making recommendations about other categories of travellers, such as students, immigrants and guest workers, who are strictly national responsibilities. Within these categories restrictive measures have been and continue to be imposed, as listed below. For whatever reasons, the countries listed in Figure 8.1 have decided that the benefits of restricting other types of visitors outweigh the costs.

Figure 8.1 is based on information available to the Panos Institute in March 1988. It may not be wholly accurate, although Panos has endeavoured to confirm the measures with the health or immigration authorities in each country. Those planning travel to foreign countries should check with officials of the country of destination for up-to-date information on current regulations.

Figure 8.1: COUNTRIES SCREENING FOREIGNERS FOR HIV

BELGIUM — Foreign students receiving scholarships from the Ministry of Foreign Affairs are tested for HIV-antibodies.

BULGARIA — All foreigners staying longer than one month, and all Bulgarians returning from working abroad, are tested for HIV-antibodies.

CHINA — All foreigners staying longer than one year must be tested for HIV-antibodies. Although visitors staying for less time are not routinely tested, those discovered to be carrying the virus are placed in isolation and deported.

COSTA RICA — Foreign students and all applicants for residence are tested for HIV-antibodies.

CUBA — Foreigners (but not tourists) and Cubans returning from AIDS-endemic areas are required to be tested on arrival for HIV-antibodies. If negative, the test is repeated six months later. Cuba is in the process of screening all its own citizens, and seropositive individuals are quarantined.

CZECHOSLOVAKIA — Foreign students are tested for HIV-antibodies.

WEST GERMANY — All students receiving a scholarship from the Ministry of Economic Co-operation are tested for HIV-antibodies. In the state of Bavaria, all foreigners applying for a residence permit, excluding nationals of the European Community and all other western European countries, must undergo a test for HIV-antibodies.

INDIA — All foreigners staying longer than a year are tested for HIV-antibodies.

IRAQ — All foreigners entering Iraq and staying longer than five days (and all Iraqis returning from abroad) must undergo testing.

KUWAIT — Numerous reports indicate that all foreigners applying for a work permit are tested although the Embassy in London denies this.

PHILIPPINES — Foreigners applying to stay longer than six months and all foreign seamen must present "AIDS-Clearance certificate" approved by the Philippine Government.

QATAR — Applicants for work permits are tested.

SAUDI ARABIA — Applicants for work permits for longer than one month are required to prove they are HIV-antibodies-free.

SOUTH AFRICA — Applicants for work permits are tested. All citizens and foreigners may be tested on demand for HIV-antibodies with foreigners subject to deportation if found positive.

SOVIET UNION — Foreign students are automatically tested for HIV-antibodies. Other foreigners (and Soviet citizens) may be tested on demand.

SYRIA — Foreign students and applicants for work permits are tested for HIV-antibodies. Syrian scholarship students returning from abroad are tested.

UNITED ARAB EMIRATES — Press reports indicate that all foreigners applying for a work permit are tested, although the embassy in London denies this.

UNITED STATES — All applicants for immigrant visas are tested for HIV-antibodies.

A number of other countries have legislation to allow exclusion of foreigners with HIV or AIDS, without requiring of specific groups. These include Indonesia and Thailand, who prohibit non-citizens with AIDS from entering the country, and Sri Lanka and South Yemen, who have been known to expel individuals with HIV or AIDS.

A number of other countries have been reported to be considering restrictions on some or all foreign visitors. Among them are Israel, Jamaica, Japan, Libya, the Republic of Korea, Papua New Guinea and Turkey.

THE ILLOGICALITY OF CONTROLS

A frequent characteristic of the controls is their inconsistency and arbitrariness, suggesting that they are indeed often motivated more by the gut reaction of blaming others than by logic or public health. Thus students and other young people are often tested, as are applicants (especially relatively unskilled applicants) for work permits: most countries can afford to exclude them. Governments have been less eager to shut out other categories of visitor: diplomats and airline personnel are not tested; businessmen and tourists are rarely tested.

The travel restrictions have so far hurt Africans most seriously, particularly several hundred students who have been expelled from countries requiring them to undergo AIDS blood tests. Many African countries rely heavily on foreign universities to train their students in the professional disciplines needed to further their economic, technological and social development. Closing this avenue to higher education to those who are HIV-positive may prove a serious setback. Few African governments can afford to retaliate by discouraging foreign tourists or investment.

The United States has decided to screen all potential immigrants; the USSR and South Africa give health authorities discretionary powers to screen all visitors. The US legislation prompted Nigerian officials to speak of possible retaliatory measures, while the USSR's move caused British authorities to request that UK citizens in the Soviet Union be exempted from testing unless certified sterile needles and syringes — sometimes in short supply in Russia — could be made available.

Seen as a hurried response to the blaming others syndrome, the controls are perhaps unsurprising. But from a public health perspective they have resulted in a number of absurdities.

The new US regulations, for example, mean that immigrants currently residing illegally in the United States face a test for the AIDS virus before they can legalise their status. A number of these immigrants — no one knows how many — will have contracted the virus in the United States, and then be expelled when they apply for legal residence and are found to be HIV-positive. A measure introduced on the grounds that the United States does not wish to import AIDS cases from the rest of the world will mean that the United States is effectively exporting AIDS.

Belgium only screens foreign students, many from Africa, receiving scholarships from one ministry; are non-scholarship students considered less likely to have been exposed to the virus?

Cuba screens nationals returning from AIDS-endemic regions, and all foreigners except tourists and the Philippines screens foreign seamen but not tourists. Does the hard currency which accompanies the tourists prevent them from picking up or passing on HIV?

India screens foreign students, though not its own students, who may have travelled abroad and exposed themselves to the virus in the very countries from which the foreign students originate.

A country with no or very few cases of AIDS is clearly most likely to become infected from abroad. And rigorous exclusion of potential carriers certainly *sounds* as if it should be a useful countermeasure against a domestic AIDS epidemic ever starting. But to be really effective it would have to involve quarantining visitors (and making sure they had no access to unsafe sex) for six months, since it can take this long before an HIV-carrier shows a positive bloodtest. Similar measures would also have to be imposed on domestic citizens returning from abroad, and also on both domestic and foreign airline crews, seamen, truck drivers, tourists and businessmen.

Such a strict policy would probably be politically, administratively and economically impossible. So the grounds for screening have often tended to be political rather than medical: intentionally or unintentionally giving official support to the concept that AIDS should be blamed on foreigners.

CHAPTER NINE

DIFFERENT PEOPLES, DIFFERENT MESSAGES

This book started by describing how AIDS, first known as a disease of white, relatively affluent homosexual men in the United States and then Europe, is increasingly hitting the peoples of Africa, the Caribbean and Latin America, and ethnic minorities in the United States. These peoples are suffering not only from AIDS itself, but also from epidemics of stigmatisation and prejudice, blame and counter-blame. *dishonor*

The war against AIDS is a global one, and one of its outstanding features is a mismatch between resources and need. Since viruses are disrespectful of human frontiers, winning this war requires that those with greater resources assist those with less. Both ethnic minorities in the North, and whole countries in the Third World, often lack the resources to employ the capital-intensive methods of AIDS treatment and control which have been adopted in richer places. But this does *not* mean that the disadvantaged must resign themselves to the passive role of victims, dependent on outside help to fight AIDS.

The AIDS pandemic is revealing — not for the first time — a fact about development which is more easily stated than taken account of: when it comes to the welfare and survival of Third World and minority communities, the only "experts" are those communities themselves.

AIDS prevention can only be effective if it changes people's sexual behaviour. In the Third World, and among ethnic minorities in the North, this is unlikely to happen if AIDS education is perceived to emanate from a predominantly white, relatively privileged, outside establishment. Instead it must be made compatible with the aspirations and plans which those communities are drawing up for their own development.

Homosexual men's organisations in the United States and Europe, several years before governments gave any support, mobilised safer sex education campaigns. They developed caring programmes for people who were HIV-positive or sick with AIDS, and for their families and loved ones. These activities were effective precisely because they were designed and implemented by homosexual men for homosexual men.

In the United States, these efforts, and the later ones of city and state health authorities, have largely failed to reach the black and hispanic ethnic minorities. This is largely because mainly white homosexual men, and mainly white city and state bureaucracies, do not have the necessary understanding of ethnic minority cultures and lifestyles. As we shall see later this in this chapter, the US ethnic minority communities are now beginning to mobilise themselves for this task.

Similarly, the style and content of government safer sex campaigns in Scandinavia or the United Kingdom are not likely to be culturally acceptable in the Caribbean or Africa. This chapter also examines the ways in which different Third World societies have been developing their own ways of educating people to protect themselves from HIV. The experience of the international family planning movement offers some interesting analogies; family planning, like AIDS prevention, requires education about sex. Early family planning campaigns in the Third World were based heavily on US and European perceptions and techniques. The message was one of population explosion and of birth control; the techniques proposed were the condom, the pill and the coil. Many such campaigns were culturally inappropriate: one foreign group, for example, hired an elephant to walk round Indian villages with slogans about condoms painted on its side.

In Zimbabwe, before independence in 1980, the family planning campaign was opposed by both the main African nationalist parties. Its stress on limiting African population growth was seen as another attempt by the ruling white minority to control the black majority; it was run mainly by men; and it focused heavily on birth control. Within a year of independence, the Mugabe government had made its own analysis of rapid population growth, and concluded that even with a fairer distribution of land it imposed impossible strains on natural resources. A new campaign was developed, planned and implemented largely by black women, and building on traditional Zimbabwean methods of child spacing. It has been very much more successful.

For AIDS as for family planning, different people require different messages. And to be most effective, those messages should ideally be designed and delivered by people from the communities which they are meant to help.

CONDOMS AND ZERO GRAZING

Tanzania already has a serious AIDS epidemic, but other than in the northwest of the country near the Ugandan border, AIDS has not yet heavily affected people in more rural areas. Although Tanzania's 1,608 reported AIDS cases (to March 1988) have received a lot of national publicity, the need for individuals to cut down on their number of sexual partners has yet to hit home, according to Tanzanian journalist Hikloch Ogola. In a recent opinion survey conducted in the capital of Dar es Salaam, 40% of those questioned recommended that condom use, accompanied by extensive health advertisements, as have appeared in the West, would constitute the most effective anti-AIDS campaign for Tanzania.[1] Twenty per cent believed that AIDS could be controlled by banning prostitution, and by instituting small-scale government work and training schemes for the young unemployed. It is noteworthy, says Ogola, that not a single interviewee even hinted that he or she was considering limiting his or her sexual relations to fewer partners. The national AIDS campaign includes some public education, and in the following article another Tanzanian journalist, Lazaro Timmo, describes the mixed local reactions.

"ONE WIFE? YOU MUST BE JOKING!"

BY
Lazaro Timmo,
Tanzanian journalist, Arusha.

When 35 year old Lenika Savorek (not his real name) read a poster explaining that to avoid infection with AIDS he should "have sex with only one faithful partner", he burst into laughter. "What am I going to do with my other wives?", he asked.

Savorek belongs to the Waarusha tribe, an ethnic group sharing a similar culture with the Masai. He has three wives. They all live in one homestead about 30km east of the town of Arusha. He thinks he might marry a fourth wife if the harvest is good next season. Wives are a reliable source of labour who look after farms and livestock, and jointly take care of the husband and children. To tell Savorek to relate to only one faithful partner is like telling him to get rid of his other wives, who are his source of wealth and prestige.

Savorek and many other people in his neighbourhood have never heard of or known any AIDS patient, so they are less worried about the disease than people in other parts of Tanzania. Their main health worry is malaria or measles, which have claimed the lives of many people they know.

In many tribes sex is not a subject which one discusses openly. Instructing someone how to do it is even more difficult. The only opportunity for elders and youth to talk freely about sex is during coming-of-age ceremonies. Girls are instructed by older women on how to handle men, while older men instruct boys. Although in theory husbands and wives are faithful to each other, as in every society throughout the world there are exceptions to that rule.

Condoms are another source of difficulty. In many villages they are unknown, and nurses often find that using euphemisms to talk about condoms confuses people rather than enlightens them. And when local people do understand, that does not mean they want to use them. "Some of those living in urban areas have heard of the condom but regard it as self-abuse to use one. They find them unnatural," said one nurse.

Condoms are easily found in towns, either on sale in shops or free from family planning organisations. Most come from the United States and have a price equivalent to 20 US cents. According to one storekeeper in Arusha, demand is increasing daily. Previously, people who needed condoms used to sneak into the shop when there were no other customers, whisper to the shop assistant and have the condom wrapped behind the counter. "It seems as if those who lead a promiscuous life have realised that it is either the condom or they perish. They now order condoms openly," he said.

Some people won't wear a condom. Twenty eight year old Daniel is a truck-driver who works between Dar es Salaam and Rwanda. "It's like a sock", he says, "and that part of the body is not meant to have socks on it."

Daniel is unhappy that truck-drivers have been blamed for spreading AIDS: he considers that everyone, not just lorry-drivers, is to blame. But he isn't particularly afraid of the disease. "It is one of the risks of life you have to face. For example my truck might break down in a dangerous place or I might have an accident. AIDS is no worse."

Besides, Daniel believes there *is* a cure for AIDS, but that it is being kept secret.

As this Tanzanian report shows, the "one partner only" recommendation can be a difficult one in parts of Africa where polygamy is an accepted basis of the traditional sexual and social order. Ugandan and Kenyan AIDS educators use the slogan "zero grazing" for just this reason, and Uganda's AIDS campaign theme, "Love Carefully", also does not specify the number of partners.

The phrase "graze at home" does not necessarily imply having just one wife, but it does mean being faithful to the wives you have. Where no one in a polygamous sexual unit is already infected with HIV, grazing at home is every bit as safe with two or three wives (or husbands) as with one, and probably safer than sleeping with one spouce and with occasional prostitutes. And if one or more individuals within the unit are already infected, grazing at home will at least confine the infection to that unit.

Zambia's efforts to alert its population to the threat of AIDS were powerfully reinforced when President Kaunda announced that his son had died of the disease — a courageous step in a society where sexually transmitted diseases, especially AIDS, are regarded as shameful. His aim in making the announcement, he said, was to raise the level of awareness about AIDS in Zambia. By early 1988, President Kaunda and President Yoweri Museveni of Uganda were still the only two heads of government anywhere in the world to have personally involved themselves in national AIDS campaigns.

Like people elsewhere, Zambians have a variety of misconceptions about AIDS and how to prevent it. Dave Moyo, a Zambian journalist on a national newspaper, who has written extensively on AIDS, investigated some of these ideas during an informal street survey of public opinion in downtown Lusaka.[2]

"THE TRUTH IS: AIDS DOESN'T EXIST"

BY
Dave Moyo,
Zambian journalist, Lusaka

Catching a sexually transmitted disease is not always seen as a serious problem in Zambia. Instead, as in so many other African countries, this is taken as a common marital hazard. Evelyn, for example, is a 50-year-old marketer living in one of Lusaka's sprawling squatter townships. She is aware that her husband has several times caught a disease. He has always visited the local clinic, but many Zambians still seek the services of local herbalists, where treatment may mask the symptoms but not completely cure the disease.

Awareness of AIDS and how to avoid it does not necessarily lead people to change their behaviour. Rose has heard of AIDS — *nthenda* in her native Nyanja tongue — through radio programmes, and now knows a little about it. Although she knows it can kill, she cannot envisage using a condom, neither would her husband think of doing so.

Beatrice, a woman in her early twenties, thinks differently. She has several "boyfriends", as well as a daughter fathered by a local executive who had promised to marry her — and she insists that her partners wear a condom. It is not always easy. "The problem is that most Zambian men are reluctant to wear condoms. They say they won't pay if they have to wear one."

Beatrice and her friends, however, have at least learned to buy condoms for themselves. "At first we were shy to go to the chemists and ask for them, but there have been all these reports about people dying from AIDS and that condoms were one way of minimising the risk of infection. We thought we had to buy them as a matter of life and death."

But Jane Chipasha, a no-nonsense hustler who offers her services for under US$2 in one of the motels in Lilanda township, still says that "skin to skin" is the most enjoyable method of making love.

The persistence of traditional beliefs are an obstacle that publicity campaigns have yet to overcome. Michael, a waiter, maintains that one can contract AIDS after having intimate sexual relations with a woman who has delivered a still-born baby. "Anybody who had sex relations with such a woman would be attacked by an incurable disease." Some Zambians are also beginning to equate AIDS with *tuyebela*, the invisible insects believed to be sent by sorcerers to cause illness. "Before the white people came to Zambia, Africans believed if a man was attacked by *tuyebela* he would not be cured," says George.

A Zambian journalist, who prefers not to be named, blames the media for much of the lack of awareness. "The local coverage of AIDS has been slanted towards trying to pinpoint where the disease comes from, and this has usually started by denying that AIDS originated in Africa. The result is that we don't present a clear picture of what AIDS is. To choose such an unpalatable opinion [that AIDS came from Africa] and start hammering on it is missing the point. The most important thing is to make people understand the seriousness of the situation."

The beliefs of Lute, a prostitute in her early 40s, confirm the ignorance that still exists. "I contracted diseases but got cured," she said. "There is no incurable disease that I contracted and there is a medicine for every disease. The truth about AIDS is that it does not exist."

PROSTITUTES PROTECT THEMSELVES

Prostitutes in a number of east and central African cities run very high risks of contracting AIDS. In Nairobi, a large group of female prostitutes live in two decrepit-looking apartment buildings, catering mainly the truck-drivers who journey from the port of Mombasa into Uganda and beyond.

In 1980, none of them tested positive for the AIDS virus. In 1983, 53% of them were HIV-positive, and by 1987 the figure had risen higher than 80%.[3]

An AIDS prevention campaign began in 1985. A public health worker spent several months meeting and getting to know the women and drew about 300 of them to a public meeting held at the end of the year. There, the women themselves decided that they needed to learn how to control and prevent AIDS. They elected a committee of community leaders, who were trained in how to motivate the others to promote condom use. Those women who had the best knowledge of AIDS prevention shared their knowledge with the others. There was group and individual counselling, where the women could discuss their problems and how to overcome them.

Elizabeth Ngugi, Kenya's chief nursing officer and a leader of the programme, has described how the women's reticence over open discussion of sex was overcome. She wrote a song to be sung at the public meetings, and to convey the basics of safer sex, the project uses role playing and dramatisation with great success.

The results have been a remarkable rise in condom use; 50% of the women insist their clients use condoms all the time and another 40% report occasional use. There has been a significant drop in the rate at which new women are becoming infected with the virus. And the women have been encouraging their clients to use condoms, too.[4]

The project, which now involves nearly 600 prostitutes, is run by the Kenya Medical Research Institute, the University of Nairobi and the Canadian University of Manitoba. It demonstrates clearly that the message itself may be less important than the way it is conveyed. But the exploitation which often accompanies Third World prostitution can create a feeling of hopelessness. In the Philippines, some of the "hospitality women" who provide "R&R" (rest and recreation) services for the US military base have already been infected with the AIDS virus. Their "working hours, drugs and lack of intellectual stimulation stagnate their ability to think about their lives", comments a social worker. "Their isolation and lack of control over their own lives instils the belief that they are powerless individuals and can only survive by complying with the demands of the bar owners and customers and/or outsmarting them." Perhaps as a result, AIDS education has so far had little impact among them in comparison with the Kenyan prostitutes.[5]

RWANDA'S NATIONWIDE CAMPAIGN

Rwanda is an East African state about the size of Switzerland, with a population of 6.8 million and the world's twelfth highest number of reported AIDS cases per capita. In 1985 the country embarked on what is so far the best-co-ordinated AIDS education campaign in the Third World. After surveying adults to find out what they knew and did not know about AIDS and how it is transmitted, the campaign co-ordinators launched a full-scale publicity effort with a series of radio programmes and the distribution of 35,000 information booklets.

Rwanda has the advantage of having a well-developed administrative and communications structure based on units ranging from districts ("prefectures") to sub-districts ("communes") and local groups ("cellules") consisting of 50 families (700 people) each. Over 60% of Rwandans can read, and each local unit is led by a person who is literate. Co-ordinated by the Rwandan Red Cross, which is well-rooted in Rwandan society at all levels, the education programme targeted first the leaders at each administrative level. They were the recipients of the AIDS booklet, and once they had read, discussed and learned it, the country was saturated with shorter and simpler leaflets on AIDS.

On picking up a leaflet, the average Rwandan could then turn to a community leader at each administrative level to ask questions or request further information. Preliminary evaluation of the programme shows that knowledge of AIDS has improved, but it is too early to tell

The Rwandan Red Cross prepared this booklet, which was sent to community leaders throughout the country. In the second stage of the education campaign, leaflets on AIDS were distributed to the whole population, who could then turn to community leaders for further information and advice.

whether changed sexual behaviour will follow. By autumn 1988, the Red Cross plans to have ready a leaflet for distribution to all Rwanda's secondary school students. Before that, however, a manual on AIDS education will be given to teachers who will be counselled about how to answer student questions on AIDS.

Rwanda's concerted programme, led by the Red Cross rather than the national AIDS committee, should soon reach every segment of society. The degree of success it achieves in slowing the spread of the AIDS virus will be of interest to all those involved in AIDS education.

AIDS AND THE CHURCHES

In Uganda, many rural people are illiterate, and the majority do not have a radio or television. So the government has had to use approaches which depend neither on the mass media nor on the ability to read. AIDS education is approached through three principal organisations: through the church, because 92% of the population attend Anglican or Roman Catholic services regularly; through the Resistance Committees found in every village; and through schools. Public meetings and political rallies are also used to spread the message. A former minister of health believes that AIDS control must be an aspect of primary health care. "AIDS is not just a doctor's business, or a nurse's business or an expert's business", he says. "Everybody, everywhere, is needed to assist in every way to spread the word on AIDS."

Both the Anglican and Roman Catholic churches in Uganda have co-operated in a government AIDS education campaign which includes the encouragement of condoms. In 1986, when Brazilian health officials were planning nationwide AIDS messages via radio, television, newspapers, posters and pamphlets, they realised that if they stressed condoms too strongly, the powerful Roman Catholic hierarchy would be sure to oppose them.

Brazilian ministry of health officials felt that groups associated with high-risk behaviour — homosexuals, bisexuals and prostitutes — needed a strong pitch for condom use. But they recognised that AIDS education in Brazil would fail if it polarised doctors and priests; the Church has a powerful influence, especially with the poor, and would be an essential channel for AIDS education.

So after careful discussions, the officials reached an accommodation with the Church: condoms could be mentioned in the AIDS advertisements as long as chastity and fidelity were given more prominence. "We made a deal with the Church", says Dr Lair

Rodrigues, head of Brazil's national AIDS programme, "and it was successful in that we were able to give Brazilians early warning about AIDS ."[7]

POP STARS, POP SONGS AND THE WORD ON AIDS

The year of AIDS education in Britain, 1987, saw the advent of a massive multi-media campaign designed to alert the public to the threat posed by the HIV virus. The campaign saw pop stars singing and talking about AIDS on radio, pulling condoms onto model penises on television programmes, and talking about their attitudes to sex on chat shows. Later in the year Richard Branson, a 38 year old British entrepreneur who launched his career by founding the Virgin records pop music company, began marketing a new brand of condoms in a blaze of publicity. Branson's links to the pop world assured that many teenagers would take note of his efforts to reduce the risk of sexual transmission of HIV through condom use.

Developing countries with a strong pop music tradition have devised their own ways of using song and the prestige of pop stars to promote AIDS education. In Guinea-Bissau in 1987 there were 23 contestants and a packed stadium for the country's first AIDS song contest. The winner of an all-expenses paid holiday to Lisbon was Buca Pussick, who sang in the local dialect of Maria, the girl with the beautiful body "who said yes to all men... after one, two, three years, she became so thin". By the end of the song the audience were all joining in the refrain: "We must be careful, this is the disease of the century. It has such power".[8]

Why is song so effective? In Guinea-Bissau, where 80% of people are illiterate, music represents one of the few avenues of communication with the potential to reach the entire population. The radio network does not cover the whole country, but a catchy pop song with a message has a good chance of circulating beyond the broadcast net via portable cassette tape decks. Music has the additional advantage of being a favourite pastime of teenagers and young adults, the group most at risk from the AIDS virus in Africa and other parts of the world.

Further south, one of Zaire's best-known singers, Franco, recorded in 1987 an album with the title "Watch out for AIDS". The title song can be heard playing not just in Kinshasa, but in record shops in Paris, London and New York, an indication of the international nature of pop music as a medium for AIDS messages.

The potential of pop music as a medium for AIDS education has only barely been tapped. Pop songs already deal with the issues which are important in conveying the facts about AIDS: romance, sex, love, faithfulness (or the lack of it), betrayal, trust and hope for the future. Francisco "Fat Boy" Costa, one of the competitors in Guinea-Bissau's contest, showed how graphically lyrics could convey the tragedy of AIDS:

"I was happy, strong and healthy
But because of an adventure
Because of a game,
Because of a senseless diversion
I have become the subject of a study".

ABORIGINES AND VOODOO

So AIDS education and prevention techniques and messages designed for majority white audiences in the industrialised countries are inappropriate and ineffective in the Third World, where each society must discover how best to influence and change sexual behaviour. Similar conclusions have been reached among ethnic minorities inside developed countries, who do not wholly share the majority culture.

Many Aborigines in Australia have a health status similar to that found in Third World countries. They face widespread malnutrition, substandard living environments and poor education. In order to reach this population with effective AIDS education, Australian community health workers have started to work with Aboriginal people, and to use established Aboriginal health worker networks. These have a practical knowledge of Aborigine culture, and a degree of recognition that visiting health workers could not achieve.

Workshops, consisting of a doctor, a nurse and communication specialists and including Aborigines, have been trying out and then adapting various messages. It was, for example, discovered in one area that "condom" was not a good word to use for the sheath, because it is similar to the name of a local tree and many Aborigine women thought they could avoid AIDS by eating its fruit. Another key point was to use red, yellow and black in leaflets: the colours of the Aborigine flag, which identifies the message as one which Aborigines can trust.

Voodoo, a traditional system of religious belief, is an important element of popular culture in Haiti. David Cueny, one of the leaders of a privately funded AIDS education campaign for the farm workers of Belle Glade, Florida (see Chapter Three), incorporated elements of voodoo belief into the AIDS messages for Haitian immigrants.

"Pamphlets failed here," says Cueny, "because so many people can't read". A better approach started with the traditional explanation of disease in voodoo: that illness is caused by a bad spirit or evil spell.

"I talk to the Haitian people about AIDS as an extremely mean spirit that tries to trick them, to make them feel well, so that they go out and spread the evil spell among the people they love. And then I teach them how to trick the spirit by practising safer sex".[9]

Cueny learned that in traditional Haitian voodoo, herb doctors and folk practitioners regularly prescribe temporary sexual abstinence as a treatment for certain ailments, so he approached them and requested their co-operation. He asked them to help prevent the spread of the AIDS virus by prescribing long-term sexual abstinence or teaching safer sexual practices. Belle Glade's AIDS programme demonstrates the labour intensive nature — talking, listening, discussing, sympathising, negotiating, explaining — of AIDS education where literacy rates are low.

AIDS AMONG US MINORITIES

As detailed in Chapter Two, both blacks and hispanics in the United States are three times as likely to have AIDS than whites. Among women, the disparity is even greater: a US black women is 13 times more likely to have AIDS than her white counterpart; a hispanic woman is eight times more likely.[10]

In August 1987 the Centers for Disease Control (CDC) convened the National Conference on AIDS and Minority Populations in Atlanta, Georgia. It brought together for the first time 800 health and social workers, community leaders and government officials. The picture that emerged was discouraging, but very clear.

"We heard about a lot of horror stories," said Dr Juan Ramos, moderator of one of the conference panels, "about an awesome accumulation of unmet needs over time, going back two or three decades." [11]

But the key message was very simple: information about AIDS is not effectively reaching US black and hispanic communities. "Those who are getting infected with the virus are not being reached by crucial information and education programmes delivered either through institutional channels or through the white, gay organisations," says Don Edwards, executive director of the National Minority AIDS Council (NMAC). "We have had to take extra pains to reverse the widespread misperception that AIDS is a white, gay, male disease and to convince government officials that a new approach to the epidemic is needed."[12]

NMAC and the National AIDS Network (NAN) are two coalitions co-ordinating around 350 of the 600 community-based organisations involved in educating US minorities on AIDS. NAN was created in 1985, and NMAC in 1986. By comparison, the Gay Men's Health Crisis (GMHC) of New York City, by far the most experienced and effective US voluntary AIDS agency, began its work in 1982. "You have to understand", said Don Edwards in late 1987, "that in the field of AIDS education, this is year six for white, gay organisations, but year one for minorities."[13]

The minority community-based organisations repeatedly stressed at the August 1987 Atlanta conference that AIDS education programmes must be designed and implemented to fit the cultural and social needs of different ethnic and social groups — and that this was not happening. In November 1987 Edwards told Panos,"What happened in the fifties with the outbreak of the polio epidemic was going to happen again. Back then vaccines were not distributed to blacks in the South in a timely manner and as a consequence they experienced a secondary epidemic. This time vital information was not being delivered to whites and minorities simultaneously."

WHY HAVE US MINORITIES DENIED THE AIDS PROBLEM?

One reason for the high incidence of HIV infection among the two main US minority communities has been the absence of government resources. Ed Pitt, director of health for the Urban League (a nationwide inter-racial organisation founded in 1910, which began to discuss AIDS earlier than most of the others) argues that the main problem is "the disproportion in the way resources are being allocated. ... The gay white leadership is controlling both the resources and the way the country reacts to the epidemic. The government does not want to allocate special resources (for combatting AIDS) to minorities. That is the racial dimension of AIDS".[14] But Don Edwards of NMAC sees it from a different angle: "Minorities have been affected by AIDS since the beginning," he says, " but instead of grabbing the bull by the horns and arguing for resources to cope with the problem, traditional groups let the gay organisations monopolise the field by default."

Many black leaders now admit that there has been unwillingness by blacks and hispanics themselves to address the problem — exactly the same phenomenon of denial that has accompanied the appearance of AIDS in every community where it has struck. AIDS has disproportionately affected people of minority origins in the United States at least since 1981, but it is only since 1987 that most prominent lobbying organisations have begun to address it. Dr Gertrude Hunter of the National Council of Negro Women acknowledges the long leg between the arrival of the virus and the dawning of recognition. "Until three years ago the image portrayed by the media was basically that AIDS was a white, gay, male disease," she told Panos in early 1988. "When they talked about AIDS among people of colour, they were referring to either Haitians or Africans. As a doctor, I knew what was going on, but it was difficult to convince black people because they go by what they get in the media."[15]

Dr Beny Primm, himself black and chairman of the Brooklyn AIDS task force in New York City, has been drawing attention to the AIDS epidemic among American minority groups for several years. Dr Primm, the only member of a minority group to sit on President Reagan's AIDS Commission, regularly warns about the dangers of denial. Black US leaders, he said in September 1987, "should not repeat the mistakes of African governments by trying to keep this problem under wraps. We must speak out, though at first we may be misunderstood even in our own communities."[16]

The fear of speaking out has been powerful, and has held back the entry of large minority coalitions into AIDS lobbying and prevention. Until 1987, much of this work was left to smaller, community-based black and hispanic organisations, some of which were created expressly to counsel and educate their people about HIV and AIDS. Under the umbrella of the National Minorities AIDS Council, these community groups, in 1986, approached the larger and longer-established minority organisations, many of them with a lengthy track record in civil rights advocacy, to participate in a national conference on AIDS and minorities. All but the Urban League declined the invitation.

Don Edwards, who is himself black, believes that "the big minority organisations didn't want to get involved at that time because it would mean talking openly about the realities of black life, about drug abuse and teen pregnancy."

Dr Wayne Greaves, chief of infectious diseases at Howard University Hospital in Washington DC, agrees: "I think blacks are afraid to speak out for fear of being identified with the problem. People feel they are betraying themselves, as blacks, by admitting that there is a problem in the black community. The community is only very slowly beginning to wake up."[17]

The latino community in the United States has similar problems. As Ruth Rodrigues of the Hispanic AIDS Forum points out, among minority communities "Nobody wants to stick their neck out".[18] Chris Jacques, a community health educator with the New York City public health department says that: "Hispanics are proud of their cultural and religious heritage, neither of which encourages them to be open about things like sex and drugs." He adds: "The denial factor was extremely high, and it definitely slowed the understanding that hispanics too were at risk." When Jacques first began to talk to hispanic community groups about AIDS in 1986, the response was: "Why are you talking to us about this? It's a disease of whites, of homosexuals and drug addicts. We don't have those kind of people here."[19]

Gilberto Gerald of the National AIDS Network puts it even more strongly: "Latino homosexuals bear such a terrible stigma ... they do not define themselves as gay although they may be having sex with other men. And an individual who tests HIV-positive would rather make up a story of intravenous drug use than admit that he has had or is having homosexual relations."[20]

Denial does not mean that homosexuality does not exist among hispanics, according to Arlene Gillespie, director of the Washington DC office of Latino Affairs, who points out that in Washington "What we have here is a lot of prostitution by young hispanic males,"[21] she says.

A professor of psychiatry at New York City's Columbia Presbyterian Hospital, Dr Rafael Tavares, explains that for hispanics to come to grips with AIDS they must talk about things which are "so taboo that they aren't even discussed among spouses". In the hispanic community there are much stricter definitions of what is acceptable behaviour for men and women, he adds: "A woman who initiates a discussion about AIDS is seen as signalling that she is a loose woman. The feeling is that if she is a good woman, she wouldn't know anything about it".[22]

Black communities, according to NMAC's Don Edwards, are still deeply suspicious of the subject of AIDS. This is confirmed by Dr Stephen Thomas, assistant professor of health education at the University of Maryland, who is conducting a survey of attitudes towards AIDS among black people in the Washington DC metropolitan area. Young blacks in the inner city, says Thomas, "perceive AIDS as some sort of germ warfare created in the government labs to be used against them. ... Past failure to deal effectively with other problems, like the war on poverty in the sixties and the war on drugs during the last two decades, adds to their disbelief when it comes to government officials telling them that now there is a war on AIDS."[23]

Thomas has also found an enormous fear of AIDS among Washington blacks — and of the victimisation and stigmatisation that is directed towards people with AIDS. Preliminary results of Professor Thomas's survey show that among government public housing residents in the Washington area, 66% agreed with the statement "It would be better to die from cancer than to live with AIDS", while 23% did not know and the rest disagreed.[24] In a nationwide Gallup poll twice as many blacks as whites (36% compared to 18%) declared themselves to be "very afraid" of contracting AIDS.[25]

Paradoxically, it is the linkage by the US Centers for Disease Control and the media of AIDS with intravenous drug use which, according to Don Edwards, has made it easier in the last two years for the large black organisations to begin to tackle AIDS. "You can almost hear a collective sigh of relief", he says, "that it's possible now to get into AIDS prevention work without confronting the issues of homosexual and bisexual behaviour". Now the big organisations are joining the National Minority AIDS Council.

USING THE GRAPEVINES

The AIDS Epidemic Among Blacks and Hispanics, a 1987 report by a multi-racial and interdisciplinary group of American AIDS researchers, comments that US ethnic minorities "know more about issues that depend upon knowledge carried by street grapevines, but are less likely to know about subjects recently promulgated through professional channels".[26] The rapidly-growing AIDS education programmes by US blacks and hispanics are focusing both on finding the appropriate message, and discovering the most effective ways of delivering it.

But building this awareness is not, they recognise, without difficulties and potential dangers: "If the data are presented only by white spokespersons, many blacks and hispanics will reject them as just another white attempt to blame minorities for the nation's troubles. If white spokespersons do not get involved, this could lead to charges that minority leaders are just engaging in special pleading and to minority criticisms of whites as not caring about AIDS among other races. In addition, there is a serious risk that whites will come to see blacks and hispanics as AIDS carriers."[27]

"We do not believe in translations", says Dr Jane Delgado, president of the National Coalition of Hispanic Health and Human Services Organizations,[28] highlighting the need to produce original AIDS education designed specifically for the hispanic community. And that is only part of the problem, because the "hispanic community" is not a homogenous body. The same approach cannot be used to reach a third generation Mexican-American who lives in Colorado, a Puerto Rican who shuttles back and forth between New York and San Juan, or an "illegal" young Guatemalan whose main preoccupation in life is not to be caught by a monster he calls *la migra*: the immigration police. Yet, all of them are at risk of contracting AIDS, and need to learn how to protect themselves.

For some communities, says Sunny Rumsey, minority outreach co-ordinator at the New York City public health department, AIDS is not even an issue. "Lack of housing, unemployment, lack of food to feed their kids... they have enough to worry about. The struggle for survival consumes all their time and their energies." [29]

And even when people have accepted that AIDS is a problem, other inhibitions remain "Hispanics are not used to talking about sex... in this population group, sex involves morals and religion," says Dr Delgado.[30] "When you talk with Latinos about how AIDS spreads", explains Arturo Olivas, director of an hispanic AIDS education project in Los Angeles, "you have to stress behaviours and avoid conceptualisations. Needle sharing is not just IV drug use, but also tattoos, or a visit with the *inyeccionista* (folk doctor who gives injections of vitamins). All these things put people at risk of contagion. For Latinos, homosexuality is simply not acceptable even for somebody involved in that type of behaviour, due to the social stigma attached to it. But 'men who have sex with other men' is recognisable.[31]

Sunny Rumsey faces the same suspicion from the groups she contacts in New York City. To try to overcome it, she uses a bilingual and bicultural team of 30 people, some ex-IV drug users and others natural leaders from the communities. "The first principle", she says, "is to build trust around you and your team and not to underestimate the people you are trying to reach. You treat a junkie from the streets with the same respect you treat a doctor. The second step is to get the right people to do the job... Outreach workers do not need master's degrees, ... [but] the willingness and the commitment to go wherever they're needed to educate their targets."[32]

Rumsey's clients are mainly intravenous drug users, whom she says are "petrified" by AIDS: eager to learn about it, to stop sharing needles or to sterilise them properly. But she warns: "No individual will really change behaviour without meaningful support... a whole set of services are lacking for the IV drug users community. Clean needles and condoms by themselves won't solve the problem and the system is totally inadequate to cope with the drug crisis."[33]

Suki Ports is a third-generation Japanese-American, and the former director of the New York City Minority Task Force on AIDS. "The difficulty does not lie in reaching people if you know how to do it and are aware of their values, their beliefs, their fears. The real problem is that top officials completely lack knowledge of the far-reaching effects of drugs and poverty and the ramifications of AIDS in that situation. Poor people are victims of the drug culture and mainstream agencies are unable or unwilling to get them out of that situation."[34]

For the US latino community, the views of the Catholic Church are extremely important. The National Conference of Catholic Bishops in Washington DC in November 1987 objected "on both moral and practical grounds" to the distribution of condoms and other contraceptives through clinics and schools, and called for federal and state governments to make this illegal. While the document deals primarily with sex education and teenage pregnancy, AIDS is not even mentioned.[35] Later that year, however, the conference's administrative board released a policy paper on AIDS which allowed that Catholic AIDS education programmes could teach that condoms give some protection against sexual transmission of the AIDS virus. Despite vocal criticism from senior conservative bishops the board has maintained its position.

Clarisa del Prado is a 42 year old Catholic from the Dominican Republic with two children. She works in the Bronx as a minority health educator with the New York City Health Department. "The Church does not help us. Look at what happened to me last November. The Bishop of the Bronx, Monsignor Francisco Jarmendia, allowed me to talk at Saint Thomas after mass. He had already made the announcement that somebody from the Department of Public Health was going to talk about AIDS. That was nice. But then he requested to see all the pamphlets I had to distribute among the people and he kept those that mentioned condoms...How can you talk about AIDS, I wonder, without talking about condoms! Of course I preach abstinence, but if I want to be realistic, I also have to talk about condoms. Finally he said he hoped I did not mind him staying during my presentation, so that he could answer people's questions. He wanted to make sure that abstinence, not condoms, would be the only message for prevention."[36]

The stress on street grapevines and person-to-person contact does not exclude more sophisticated means of communication. "*Ojos que no ven*" (Eyes that do not see) is a video soap-opera produced by the Instituto Familiar de La Raza in San Francisco to educate the Latino community on AIDS. Its characters include Doña Rosa, her homosexual son, a bisexual man who hides his condition from his wife and has an HIV-positive male sexual partner, and a newly arrived immigrant who goes with a prostitute and uses drugs.

CROSSING THE THRESHOLD OF FEAR

There is a group of people who have been forced to confront the darkest aspects of the pandemic from the firing line. They are the people with AIDS (PWAs) and those who know they are carrying the virus (seropositives). In several countries they have organised and are carrying out some of the best AIDS education programmes yet devised.

Richard Rector is a 31 year old Californian PWA who was first diagnosed in 1982. His work as an AIDS educator began in 1986, after a failed suicide attempt and a subsequent period of depression and withdrawal led him to a decision which has since guided his life. He realised that he had a choice: he could play the role of victim, trapped in a cycle of misery, anger, resentment and helplessness, or he could fight for both himself and others, and in so doing make the rest of his life as meaningful as possible. He chose the latter and decided to use his experience as both as a PWA and as an active member of local and national PWA organisations to form the basis of a new career as an AIDS educator.

Working first for a county health department in California, he later criss-crossed the United States to assess the support services available for PWAs and seropositives. Invited by the Norwegian Government to speak at a major conference on AIDS in August 1987, he has also advised a number of European AIDS groups and, as a consultant to the Norwegian Red Cross, travelled to Africa to participate in meetings where AIDS community-based education programmes were begun.

Rector believes that PWAs and seropositives have been under-utilised in the battle against AIDS. In every AIDS-affected community he says, there are PWAs and seropositives who possess two key pieces of knowledge: they know the community they come from, how it thinks, acts and reacts; and their understanding of what it is like to have contracted the virus and be made ill by it is not based on hearsay, horror-stories or headlines, but on personal experience. In the interview which follows Richard Rector explains how his own experiences as a PWA and a member of the US National Association of People with AIDS (NAPWA) have shaped his views about the ways in which the barriers of ignorance and prejudice which surround the subject of AIDS can best be surmounted.

> "To be a PWA or a seropositive person is to be concerned with discrimination. It surfaces in every aspect of your daily life and in your relationships. Yet in my travels I have been surprised by the extent to which the human experience of AIDS is the same wherever I go. Whether in North America, Europe or Africa, people have responded to me as a PWA in similar ways. They haven't reacted to me as someone belonging to a dangerous 'risk group', but as a person. Their grief over friends or relatives who have died of AIDS has affected them deeply, no matter where they are from. Their conditions may be different, but the emotions they express are the same".

"Why then has AIDS provoked so much labelling and victimisation, particularly between different social and racial groups?"

"What strikes me is that, until people are personally touched by AIDS, either by getting sick themselves or seeing friends or family members become seropositive, they just don't give a damn. They are content to fall back on all the old rationalisations that their own group or community is 'safe', and that someone else is at risk and at fault and deserving of, at best, benign neglect and at worst punishment or forced isolation.

"Even where there are no obvious divisions based on race, sex, or class, discrimination occurs. In NAPWA we had a long battle to convince the organisation that it should include seropositive people as well as PWAs. Can you imagine? — the PWAs felt that their situation was unique and for a long time wanted to exclude seropositives. Those in favour of inclusion had to demonstrate that seropositives suffered at least as much discrimination as PWAs. But the point is that we did keep discussing until the doors were opened."

"Why do you believe that PWAs have a special role to play in overcoming these attitudes?"

"For one thing, PWAs have crossed a certain fear threshold. They already have the disease which scares everyone half to death. They've had to learn to live with that fear and many of them have transcended it. Even though I'm a PWA myself, over and over again I've been impressed by how open and unafraid so many PWAs are. You can't help but be impressed. We can help people to learn to overcome the fear which blinds them to the realities of AIDS.

"Secondly, seeing or meeting a PWA humanises the whole situation. That PWA could be your son, your brother, your sister or your friend. It makes it harder to argue that 'AIDS victims' and seropositive people should be locked up somewhere out of sight. In my travels I have found that, while many people seem to believe that repressive measures must be enacted to deal with AIDS, they would always say to me: 'But of course Richard, you are an exception'. They could only support harsh methods as long as the object of discrimination remained a faceless, stereotyped 'victim' whom they could blame at a distance. That's probably why Haiti, and then Africa, have been seen in the United States as likely sources of AIDS."

"So are you saying that being a PWA, or knowing a PWA, somehow automatically makes you more free of prejudice than the average person?"

"No, and it's interesting how we've had to wrestle with issues of discrimination within NAPWA. It's a national organisation, and it reflects all the well-known geographic, social, racial and sexual divisions which are found in society at large. We've had to overcome the tendency to factionalism: you know, the east Coast group versus the west coast group; the northern Californians versus the southern Californians; the old guard, mainly gay men who've been in NAPWA for four or five years, versus the newcomers, not all gay, who have a variety of different ideas, styles and methods; and of course, PWAs of colour versus white PWAs."

"How did the racial tensions surface?"

"Well, NAPWA was founded in 1983 and for some time was composed of white gay men. It was the Reverend Charles Angel, a black minister and PWA from New York City, who first challenged us about what he called our 'non- inclusion' of black people and their concerns. He would say things like: 'This really looks like a purely gay, white, male organisation to me. Where are the people of colour? They have AIDS, but for all your talk about combating discrimination, you are neglecting them'. As a result we had some pretty intense discussions."

"Acrimonious discussions?"

"Heated, but, well, nobody stomped out of the room or anything. We stayed and talked it out. And in the end we all learned a lot about our human tendency to focus exclusively on the needs of our own group while forgetting about others in need."

"How do you deal with what might be called the 'denial syndrome', the fear which leads to so much casting of blame?"

"Of course, one of the trickiest things about denial is that at the time you don't realise you're doing it! Let me give you an example. In September 1986 the board of directors of NAPWA

142

had 11 members. By the end of October that year, there were only three left. Eight members had died of AIDS in the interval. Throughout that two month period I was in charge of the meetings and I would call them to order, proceeding through the agenda just as if nothing had happened. I wouldn't speak about or refer to the missing members. Then one day one of the remaining few blew up at me. 'You should stop this', he said, 'you are oppressing all of us by this behaviour'. They wanted to acknowledge those who had died and grieve for them, while I was steadfastly denying that anything unusual was happening.

"This may be hard to believe, but it's true, and it shows how deeply rooted is our tendency to deny things we feel we can't cope with until someone else calls us up on them. Because of this experience I can understand why many countries in the past have said 'We don't have AIDS, it's a Western disease', or 'We have AIDS, but it came from Africa', or whatever. Denial is a normal response and we must struggle both to recognise it is happening and to overcome it.

"Can PWAs help to forge links between different groups affected by AIDS? For example, would NAPWA on the one hand and, say, PWA groups in Africa, or Haiti, or Latin America, benefit by communicating with one another?"

"I believe that not only they, but society at large will benefit. PWAs and seropositives need, above all, to find acceptance, trust, and safety. Being victimised and alienated by one's society not only causes psychological stress, but many PWAs feel it makes the physical illness worse too. We can find a safe place only when more and more of us come forward to tell our story. Then people will stop thinking of us as a faceless 'risk group'. More than anything else, PWAs are conscious that, whatever divides us, our common enemy is AIDS, not each other. PWAs can provide the missing human element in AIDS education campaigns."[37]

CHAPTER TEN

CONCLUSIONS

This book has deliberately set out to examine a touchy subject. It seems that both as individuals and as societies, we all have a tendency first to deny the existence of a frightening problem, and then to blame someone else for causing it. The effects of blame, in all its forms, are negative, sowing confusion and victimising the least powerful: only the virus profits from this. Still, almost every society affected by AIDS seems to have danced the same futile minuet of blame and counter-blame.

The way that AIDS is increasingly affecting people of colour in the United States, the indications that many AIDS epidemics in the Third World are at present under-estimated, the important debate on the origins of the HIV virus, the possibility that ethnic groups vary in their vulnerability to AIDS, discussion of prostitution and promiscuity in various societies: these issues have all been muddied by the casting of blame — or by the belief that blame is being unjustly or malevolently cast by others. AIDS has been successively used to direct blame, stigmatisation and prejudice at homosexual men, prostitutes, intravenous drug users, Haitians, African students in the USSR and India, blacks and hispanics in the United States, US seamen in the Philippines, foreigners in Japan, Europeans in Africa ... the examples vary, but the stigmatisation does not.

In *Blaming Others*, Panos has wherever possible drawn on the views and judgments of scientists, spokespersons and writers from the Third World, and from minority communities in the North. This book has endeavoured to document these epidemics of blame as dispassionately as possible, leaving it to the reader to judge when individuals or nations have really been behaving in a racist manner, or when a denunciation of blame from outside has been a convenient way of continuing to ignore the real problem of AIDS in a society or community. The book has not set out to blame the blamers, but rather to document the totally counter-productive impact of blame on individuals, groups and AIDS campaigns.

AIDS is unlike all other health challenges in many ways; one key difference is that until the development of a vaccine and of cheap and widespread treatment, virtually the only effective weapon we have against it is persuading people to change their sexual behaviour. AIDS prevention means AIDS education, and AIDS education means talking about sex: our own and other people's. We all have to learn to do this without giving and taking offence.

So far, the global response to AIDS, and most of the national responses, have been dominated by the experience and the cultural assumptions of white middle class people from North America and Europe. This is beginning to change, and *Blaming Others* has also documented the growing awareness of people in many societies and cultures that they must develop their own approaches to AIDS. Different peoples need different messages.

Kenya's "zero grazing", Uganda's "love carefully", safer sex in the United States, the Brazilian church-supported campaign stressing chastity as well as condoms, Rwanda's radio programmes, the UK's discussion of AIDS on TV chat-shows, Guinea-Bissau's pop-song contest: there is encouraging evidence that if we cannot yet claim to be *winning* the battle against AIDS, we are at least beginning to fight it more intelligently and sensitively.

In retrospect it is unfortunate that public health workers, governments and the media in many countries have identified various "risk groups" for AIDS. Homosexual men, intravenous drug users, haemophiliacs, Haitians, Africans, prostitutes, foreigners, blacks: the labels vary but the results do not. One effect has been to legitimise the blame, prejudice and discrimination which this book has described.

Another effect has been to suggest that anyone who does not belong to one of these groups is safe — and that AIDS only happens to people in risk groups to which the majority does not belong. The whole concept of risk groups has been used to justify a withdrawal of compassion and concern for people with AIDS.

Perhaps the single most effective counter to this attitude is Zambian President Kenneth Kaunda's assertion, mentioned earlier, that "what is more important than knowing where this disease came from is where it is going". And Dr S.I.Okware, head of Uganda's AIDS committee, said the same thing: "There is a snake in the house. Do you just sit and ask where the snake came from?"

Increasingly, public health workers are no longer confusing the snake with the person it has bitten; now, they are using the term "risk activity" rather than "risk group". Certain risk activities, such as transfusions with unscreened blood, are relatively easy to prevent, although this can be expensive and it is not being achieved fast enough. Other risk activities, such as the sharing of needles among intravenous drug users, are equally easy to identify but far harder to prevent, because nearly all societies have so far preferred to condemn such activity rather than to reduce its risks.

But the overwhelming risk activity which transmits the AIDS virus, and which is soon likely to boost the AIDS death toll into the millions, is far more common, and far more difficult to change: a sexual life-style that involves frequent partner changes, and which has been adopted by many individuals all over the world, especially in cities.

Should AIDS education aim at modifying such behaviour, by encouraging more use of condoms, or less penetrative sex, or greater faithfulness to one or a few sexual partners? Or should education aim at a broader understanding of the cultural standards, the social conditions and the economic forces which give rise to "fast-track" sex?

Blaming Others assumes that both approaches are needed, but that too little attention has so far been paid to the latter. Underdevelopment and uneven development, in the cities and rural areas of the Third World, and among the urban poor and the ethnic minorities of the United States and Europe, create the conditions in which high risk activities will flourish: intravenous drug use, injections by unqualified or incompetent medical practitioners, prostitution, unprotected sex with many partners. These same conditions impede the flow of AIDS information to those whose ignorance puts them unknowingly at risk.

In the short term, AIDS control necessarily concerns itself with emergency measures: the screening of blood used for transfusion, the sterilisation of injection equipment, the teaching of safer sex, the distribution of condoms or needle exchange schemes for intravenous drug users. But bringing the pandemic under control will require vigilant effort not for just a few months or years, but for as long as it takes to develop a vaccine or cure — perhaps a decade or even longer.

The conclusion urged by the evidence presented in *Blaming Others* is that successful AIDS prevention will require, in addition to expedient measures, deep-acting remedies. The promotion of safer sex and condom use is essential, but are not efforts to understand and tame the unchecked epidemic of sexually transmitted diseases other than AIDS in the Third World equally so? The education of prostitutes in methods of AIDS avoidance is urgent, but where are the programmes of social and economic support for prostitutes who simply cannot find less dangerous and demoralising work? Providing clean needles for intravenous drug users may save them from the AIDS virus now, but is this such a great victory if they die prematurely anyway, of overdose or drug-associated illness?

Like a misery-seeking missile, AIDS is homing in on a global underclass. But from the hundreds of thousands of individual tragedies which make up the worldwide tragedy of AIDS there is perhaps one benefit to be derived: it may eventually force international attention to the vulnerability caused by unbalanced development, both between rich and poor nations, and within our individual societies. The great challenge of AIDS is not only to outsmart a new virus — though this task is one of unprecedented scientific and organisational complexity —- but to comprehend and change the vulnerabilities which provide the virus with such fertile soil. That this comprehension and change requires the full engagement of the vulnerable communities themselves, in an atmosphere free from blame and stigmatisation, is the single most important message of this book.

REFERENCES

CHAPTER ONE: AIDS AND RACE: WHY IT MATTERS

1. R.W. Smith, "The national impact of negativistic leadership", presented at the 1987 Meeting of the Western Political Sciences Association, Arnheim, 26-28 March 1987.

2. J. Mann, statement to the UN General Assembly, 20 October 1987, New York.

3. WHO communiqué, number 50, November 1987.

CHAPTER TWO: A DISEASE OF DISADVANTAGE

1. J. W. Curran et al, "Epidemiology of HIV Infection and AIDS in the United States", **Science**, 5 February 1988, volume 239, pp 610-6.

2. J. W. Curran et al, op. cit.

3. **New York Times**, 14 February 1988.

4. **AIDS Newsletter**, 19/1988.

5. R. Hoff et al, "Seroprevalence of Human Immunodeficiency Virus among childbearing women: estimation by testing samples of blood from newborns", **New England Journal of Medicine**, 3 March 1988, volume 318, no. 9, pp 525-530.

6. **International Herald Tribune,** 14 January 1988.

7. J. W. Pape et al, "Pattern of HIV infection in Haiti, 1977-1986", **Abstracts of the International Conference on AIDS**, Washington, 1987, p 6.

8. M. Merlin et al, "Infection by HIV among populations of six countries of Central Africa" **Abstracts of the International Conference on AIDS**, Washington, 1987, p 5.

9. **New York Times**, 14 February 1988.

10. D. R. Hopkins, address to National Conference on AIDS in Minority Populations in the United States, 8 August 1987

11. **Morbidity and Mortality Weekly Report**, 15 May 1987, volume 36, no 18, pp 273-276.

12. Report of the Secretary's Task Force on Black and Minority Health, Department of Health and Human Services, Washington DC, US Government Printing Office, 1987-0-174-719, August 1985, pp63-86.

13. **AIDS and People of Color: the Discriminatory Impact**, AIDS Discrimination Unit of the New York City Commission on Human Rights, August 1987 (updated), p 3.

14. Speech delivered by US. Surgeon-General C. Everett Koop before the Presidential Advisory Commission on HIV, 9 September 1987.

15. A. M. Hardy et al, "Review of death certificates to assess completeness of AIDS case reporting", **Public Health Report**, July/August 1987, volume 102, pp 386-91.

16. Interview with Dr Jonathan Mann, head of Global Programme on AIDS, World Health Organization, April 1988.

17. Interview with Dr Ron St John, Co-ordinator, Health Situation and Travel Assessment Program, Pan American Health Organization, January 1988.

18. P. Piot et al, "AIDS: An International perspective", **Science**, 5 February 1988, volume 239, pp 573-9.

19. J. Mann, AIDS epidemiology, impact, prevention and control: the WHO perspective, statement read by Dr O. T. Christiansen to the German Marshall Fund of the United States Conference, West Berlin, 25-27 June, 1987.

20. Anonymous, "AIDS in Africa", **AIDS-Forschung**, January 1987, Volume 1, pp 5-25; P. Piot et al, op cit.

21. J. M. Mann et al, "Surveillance for AIDS in a central African City: Kinshasa Zaire", **Journal of American Medicine**, 20 June 1986, volume 255, number 23, pp 3255-9.

22. J. W. Curran et al, op cit.

23. P. Piot et al, op cit.

24. Dr Leonardo Mata, interview, October 1987.

25. **Abstracts of the Second International Symposium on AIDS and Associated Cancers in Africa**, Naples, October 1987.

26. P. Piot et al, op cit.

27. J. Mann, statement given in an informal briefing to the 42nd session of the UN General Assembly, 20 October 1987.

28. Ibid.

29. P. Piot et al, op cit; R. M. Anderson et al, "Possible demographic consequences of AIDS in developing countries", **Nature**, 17 March 1988, volume 332, number 6161, pp 228-234.

30. C. Meyers, Presentation on the Social and Economic Impact of AIDS in Developing Countries, Third International Conference on AIDS, Washington DC, June 1987.

31. B. M. Nkowane, "Implications of the Human Immunodeficiency Virus (HIV) and the acquired immunodeficiency syndrome (AIDS) for primary industry", Abstracts of the First International Conference on the Global Impact of AIDS, London, March 1988, p 35.

32. F. Davichi et al, "Economic Impact on families of children with AIDS

in Kinshasa, Zaire", Abstracts of the First International Conference on the Global Impact of AIDS, London, March 1988, p 36.

33. Quoted in **South** magazine, London, December 1987.

34. Randy Shilts, **And The Band Played On**, New York: St Martin's Press, 1987, 630pp.

35. Larry Kramer, **The Normal Heart**, New York City, 1985.

CHAPTER THREE: PORTARAITS OF VULNERABILITY

1. "AIDS surveillance update, February 14, 1987", New York City Department of Health AIDS Surveillance Unit.

2. David N. Dinkins, Testimony before the select committee on narcotics of the US House of Representatives, 27 July 1987.

3. Interview, November 1988.

4. Personal communication from Dr Jean William Pape, March 1988.

5. Interview with Dr Wilson Carswell, April 1988.

6. Paper on AIDS epidemiology in the Philippines presented by Dr Virginia Basaca at the Fist International Conference on AIDS and other Sexually Transmitted Diseases in Asia, Manila, November 1987.

7. J.K. Kreiss et al "AIDS virus infection in Nairobi prostititues", **New England Journal of Medicine**, 13 February 1986, volume 314, number 7, pp414-18.

8. P. Piot et al "AIDS: an international perspective", **Science,** 15 February 1988, volume 239 pp 573-579.

9. Thai Ministry of Health statistics, October 1987, quoted in **The Nation**, Bangkok, 6 December 1987.

10. B.A. Brink et al "HIV antibody prevalence in migrant mineworkers in South Africa during 1986" **Abstracts of the International Conference on AIDS**, Washington, June 1987, p6.

11. Undated paper "Mass testing shows no proven case of AIDS on mines", published by The South African Chamber of Mines in 1986, p2.

12. **Financial Times**, London, 5 September 1987.

13. Interview, September 1987.

CHAPTER FOUR: ORIGINS OF AIDS ORIGINS OF BLAME

1. US Centers for Disease Control: "Pneumocystic pneumonia - Los Angeles", **Morbidity and Mortality Weekly Report**, 5 June 1981, volume 30, number 21, pp 250-2; and M. S. Gottlieb et al, "Pneumocystis carinii pneumonia and mucosal candidiasis in previously healthy homosexual men", **New England Journal of Medicine,** 10 December 1981, volume 305, number. 24, pp 1425-1431.

2. For a narrative account of the dawning awareness of a new immunodeficiency disease in the US see Randy Shilts, **And The Band Played On,** New York: St Martin's Press, 1987, 630pp.

3. B. Lamey and N. Malemeka, "Aspects cliniques et epidémiologiques de la cryptococcose à Kinshasa", **Médecine Tropicale**, September-October 1982, volume 42, number 5, pp 507-11.

4. A. C. Bayley, "Aggressive Kaposi's sarcoma in Zambia, 1983", **Lancet,** 16 June 1984, pp 1318-20.

5. **Morbidity and Mortality Weekly Report**, J. Vandepitte et al, "AIDS and cryptococcosis (Zaire, 1977)", **Lancet**, 23 April 1983, pp 925-6.

6. G. Offenstadt et al, "Multiple opportunistic infection due to AIDS in a previously healthy black woman from Zaire", **New England Journal of Medicine,** 31 March 1983, volume 308, p 775.

7. R. J. Biggar et al (edit), "Epidemiology of AIDS in Europe" and following articles, **European Journal of Cancer and Clinical Oncology,** 1984, volume 20, number 2, pp 157-73; N. Clumeck et al, "Acquired immune deficiency syndrome in Black Africa", **Lancet,** 19 March 1983, p 642; J. B. Brunet and R. A. Ancelle, **Annals of Internal Medicine,** "The international occurence of the acquired immunodeficiency syndrome", November 1985, volume 103, number 5, pp 670-4.

8. J. W. Pape et al, "Characteristics of the acquired immunodeficiency syndrome (AIDS) in Haiti", **New England Journal of Medicine**, 20 October 1983, volume 309, number 16, pp 945-50.

9. "Opportunistic Infections and Kaposi's Sarcoma among Haitians in the United States", **Morbidity and Mortality Weekly Report**, 9 July 1982, volume 31, number 26, pp 353-361.

10. **Chicago Tribune,** 25 October 1987.

11. T. Jonckheer et al, "Cluster of HTLV-III/LAV infection in an African family", **Lancet**, 16 February 1985, pp 400-1.

12. J. Vandepitte et al, op cit.

13. C. Bygbjerg, "AIDS in a Danish Surgeon (Zaire, 1976)", **Lancet**, 23 April 1983, pp 925.

14. **Chicago Tribune,** Ibid.

15. **Chicago Tribune,** Ibid.

16. G. Williams et al, "Cytomegalic Inclusion Disease and Pneumocystis carinii Infection in an Adult", **Lancet**, 29 October 1960, pp 951-955.

17. G. R. Hennigar et al, "Pneumocystis Carinii in an Adult", **American Journal of Clinical Pathology**, April 1961, volume 35, number 4, pp 353-64.

18. R. J. Biggar et al, "Regional variation in prevalance of antibody against human t-lymphotropic virus types I and III in Kenya, East Africa", **International Journal of Cancer**, 15 June 1985, volume 35, pp 763-7; W.

C. Saxinger et al, "Evidence for exposure to HTLV-III in Uganda before 1973", **Science,** 1 March 1985, volume 227, pp 1036-38.

19. D. Serwadda et al, "Slim disease: a new disease in Uganda and its association with HTLV-III infection", **Lance**t, 19 October 1985, pp 849-52; R. J. Biggar, "The AIDS Problem in Africa", **Lancet,** 11 January 1986, pp 79-83; J. W. Carswell et al, "How Long Has The AIDS Virus Been In Uganda?" **Lancet,** 24 May 1986, p 1217.

20. Personal communication, Dr Richard Tedder, March 1988.

21. Interview with Dr Michael Adler, November 1984.

22. The British approach, based on the use of the competitive ELISA antibody test, and the reasons for its adoption are discussed in: R Tedder, **Bulletin Institut Pasteur**, 1986, number. 84, pp 405-413.

23. Interview, April 1988.

24. **Chicago Tribune,** 25 October 1987.

25. A. J. Nahmias et al, "Evidence for Human Infection with an HTLV III/LAV-Like Virus in Central Africa, 1959", **Lancet**, 31 May 1986, pp 1279-80.

26. R. Shilts, op cit.

27. W. A. Pusey, **The History and Epidemiology of Syphilis,** Springfield, Illinois and Baltimore, Maryland, 1933.

28. The possibility that the AIDS virus may have through the unforeseen genetic recombination of two or more labratory microbes is not discussed in this chapter, since such a possibility has seldom been raised in popular or published scientific discussion of origins.

29. **Guardian**, London, 5 October 1987.

30. "Guidelines for the development of a national AIDS prevention and control programme", World Health Organization, Special Programme on AIDS, October 1987; interview with Dr. J. M. Mann, **African Concord**, 29 January 1988, pp 31-34.

31. **Morbidity and Mortality Weekly Report**, op cit.

32. **New York Times**, 3 July 1983.

33. R. S. Greco, "Haiti and the stigma of AIDS", **Lancet**, 27 August 1983, pp 515-6.

34. **Washington Post,** 2 August 1983.

35. Personal communication.

36. **Miami Herald**, 24 December 1983.

37. J. Teas, "Could AIDS Agent be a New Variant of African Swine Fever Virus?" **Lancet,** 23 April 1983, p 923.

38. J. Vieira, "The Haitian Link" in V. Gong, **AIDS: Facts and Issues**, New Brunswick and London, Rutgers University Press, pp 117-23.

39. **New York Times**, 29 July 1983.

40. "Update: Acquired Immunodeficiency Syndrome -- United States", **Morbidity and Mortality Weekly Report**, 10 May 1985, volume 34, number 18, pp 245-248.

41. **Haitian Refugees in the US,** Minority Rights Group Report number 52, London, January 1982, 20pp.

42. **New York Times**, 28 June 1983.

43. **AIDS and People of Color: the Discriminatory Impact**, the AIDS Discrimination Unit of the New York City Commission on Human Rights, August 1987, pp 23-4.

44. **New York Times**, 29 November 1983 and 11 October 1984.

45. F. Cineas, "Haitian ambassador deplores AIDS connection", **New England Journal of Medicine**, 15 September 1983, volume 309, number 11, pp 668-9.

46. N. Clumeck et al, **Lancet**, op cit; N. Clumeck et al, "Acquired immunodeficiency syndrome in African patients", **New England Journal of Medicine,** 23 February 1984, volume 310, pp 492-7; J. B. Brunet et al, "Acquired immunodeficiency in France", **Lancet,** 26 March 1983, pp 700-1.

47. Kevin M. de Cock, " AIDS: an old disease from Africa?" **British Medical Journal**, 4 August 1984, volume 289, pp 306-8; see also ensuing BMJ correspondence.

48. **New York Times**, 8 November 1985.

49. R. J. Biggar et al, **International Journal of Cancer**, op cit

50. W. C. Saxinger et al, "Evidence for exposure to HTLV-III in Uganda before 1973", op cit.

51. R. J. Biggar et al, **International Journal of Cancer,** op cit; D. Serwadda et al, op cit.

52. R. Tedder, **Bulletin Institut Pasteur**, 1986, number 84, pp 405-13.

53. **Los Angeles Times**, 22 February 1985.

54. For example see: J. A. Levy et al, "Absence of antibodies to the human immunodeficiency virus in sera from Africa prior to 1975", **Proceedings of the National Academy of the Sciences**, October 1986, volume 83, number 20, pp 7935-7; S. F. Lyons et al, "Lack of evidence of HTLV-III endemicity in Southern Africa", **New England Journal of Medicine**, 9 May 1985, volume 312, number 19, pp 1257- 8; Anonymous, "AIDS in Africa", **AIDS Forschung**, 1 January 1987, volume 1, pp 5-25.

55. A. J. Nahmias et al, op cit.

CHAPTER FIVE: GREEN MONKEYS AND GERM WARFARE

1. See especially E.N. Pavlovsky, **Natural Nidality of Transmissable Disease**, English translation edited by N.D. Levine, translations by F.K.

Plous Jr., Urbana, Illinois and London: University of Illinois Press, 1966, pp 260.

2. **Control of Communicable Diseases in Man,** American Public Health Association, 9th edition, 1960.

3. N.J. Dimmock and S.B. Primrose, **Introduction to Modern Virology,** London: Blackwell, 1987, p 307.

4. R.C. Chirimuuta and R.J. Chirimuuta, **AIDS, Africa and Racism,** Bretby, Derbyshire: R.C. Chirimuuta, 1987, p 71; available from Bretby House, Stanhope, Bretby, Nr Burton-on- Trent, Derbyshire, DE15 OPT, UK.

5. R.V. Henrickson et al, "Epidemic of acquired immunodeficiency in rhesus monkeys", **Lancet,** 19 February 1983, pp 388-90.

6. M.D. Daniel et al, "Isolation of t-cell tropic HTLV-III- like retrovirus from macaques", from **Papers from Science, 1982-1985,** Washington: The American Association for the Advancement of Science, pp 484-489; also P.J. Kanki et al, "Serologic identification and characterization of a macaque T-lymphotropic retrovirus closely related to HTLV-III", from **Papers from Science, 1982-1985,** Washington: The American Association for the Advancement of Science, pp 490-95.

7. P.J. Kanki et al, "Antibodies to simian T-lymphotropic retrovirus type III in African green monkeys and recognition of of STLV-III viral proteins by AIDS and related sera", **Lancet,** 8 June 1985, pp 1330-2; P.J. Kanki et al, "Isolation of T- lymphotropic retrovirus related to HTLV-III/LAV from wild-caught African green monkeys", **Science,** 22 November 1985, volume 230, number 4728, pp 951-4.

8. F. Barin et al, "Serological evidence for virus related to simian t-lymphotropic retrovirus III in residents of West Africa", **Lancet,** 21-28 December 1985, pp 1387-89.

9. **Le Monde,** Paris, 11/12 October 1987.

10. J.A.Levy et al, **Proceedings of the National Academy of Science, Medical Sciences,** USA, October 1986, vol 83, pp 7935- 37.

11. B.M. Traoré, "Rien ne prouve une origine Africaine du SIDA", **Jeune Afrique,** Dakar, May 1987, number 37.

12. J.W. Carswell et al, "How long has the AIDS virus been in Uganda?" **Lancet,** 24 May 1986, p 1217.

13. R.C. Chirimuuta and R.J. Chirimuuta, op cit, p 135.

14. P.J. Kanki et al, **Science,** op cit.

15. S. Giunta and G. Groppa, "The primate trade and the origin of AIDS viruses", **Nature,** 3 September 1987, volume 329, p 22.

16. R.M. Hendry et al, "Antibodies to simian immunodeficiency virus in African green monkeys in Africa in 1957-62", **Lancet,** 23 August 1986, p 455.

17. J. Green and D. Miller, **AIDS: The Story of a Disease,** London:

Grafton, 1986, p 66; quoted in R.C. Chirimuuta and R.J. Chirimuuta, op cit, p 72

18. J. Teas, "Could AIDS agent be a new variant of African swine fever virus?" **Lancet**, 23 April 1983, p 923.

19. See for example **New York Native**, 6-19 May 1985 and 14 September 1987.

20. A. Kashamura, **Famille, Sexualité, et Culture: Essai sur les Moeurs Sexuelles et les Cultures des Peuples des Grands Lacs Africains,** Paris: Payot, 1973, p 137.

21. F. Noireau, "HIV transmission from monkey to man", **Lancet**, 27 June 1987, pp 1498-9.

22. **New Scientist,** London, 16 July 1987.

23. See for example "Department of defence" in the **New York Review of Books**, 8 October 1987, pp35-7.

24. **Sunday Times of Kenya**, Nairobi, 28 June 1987.

25. For example see discussion on pp 1-8 in D. Gazi, **AIDS: the Myths and the Facts**, London: 1987, pp80.

26. J.Segal, L.Segal and R.Dehmlow, **AIDS: its Nature and Origin**, date and place of publication unknown, pp52.

27. "The USSR's AIDS disinformation campaign", July 1987, Washington: Department of State, pp14.

28. **Social Change and Development**, September 1986, number 14, p 34*.

29. **The African Interpreter**, Lagos, October 1986, number 114, pp 13-15.

30. **Blitz**, India, 7 February 1987*.

31. **Sunday Times of Kenya**, Nairobi, 21 June, 1987; **Le Devoir**, Dakar, July 1987*.

32. **Mirror**, Accra, 4 April 1987*.

33. **El Nuevo Diario**, Managua, 6 July 1987*.

34. **Sunday Mail**, Harare, 7 September 1987*.

35. Personal communication, October 1987.

36. **Jeune Afrique**, Dakar, 18 March 1987.

37. Reuters news bulletin, 30 October 1987.

38. **Izvestia**, Moscow, 30 October 1987.

*Asterisked references come from the US Department of State's report

CHAPTER SIX: SEX AND RACE

1. R. Anderson and R. May, "Plotting the spread of AIDS", **New Scientist**, March 1987, volume 26, pp 54-59.

2. O.P. Arya and J.B. Lawson, " Sexually transmitted diseases in the tropics. Epidemiological, diagnostic, therapeutic, and control aspects", **Tropical Doctor**, April 1977, volume 7, pp 51- 6.

3. P. Piot and A. Meheus, "Epidémiologie des maladies sexuellement transmissibles dans les pays en développement", **Annals de la Société Belge de Médecine Tropicale**, 1983, volume 63, pp 87-110.

4. Ibid.

5. A. O. Osoba, "Sexually transmitted diseases in tropical Africa: a review of the present situation," **British Journal of Venereal Diseases**, 1981, volume 57, pp 89-94.

6. Ibid.

7. A. O. Osoba, op. cit.

8. P. Piot and A Meheus, op. cit.

9. O. P. Arya and J.B. Lawson, op. cit.

10. "Infertility and sexually-transmitted disease: A public health challenge", **Population Reports**, July 1983, series L, number 4, pp 113-151.

11. W. Cates, et al, "Worldwide patterns of infertility: is Africa different?" **Lancet**, 14 September 1985, pp 596-8.

12. O. Frank, "Infertility in sub-Saharan Africa: Estimates and Implications", **Population and Development Review**, 1 March 1983, volume 9, number 1, pp 137-44.

13. O.P. Arya and J.B. Lawson, op. cit.

14. A.O. Osoba, op. cit.

15. Quoted in A. M. Brandt, **No Magic Bullet**, New York and Oxford: Oxford University Press, 1987, p 13.

16. Ibid, p 31.

17. A. O. Osoba, op. cit.

18. O. P. Arya and F. J. Bennett, "Role of the medical auxiliary in the control of sexually transmitted diseases in a developing country", **British Journal of Venereal Diseases**, 1976, volume 52, pp 116-21.

19. O. Frank, op cit, p 141.

20. For a recent example see Randy Shilts, **And The Band Played On**, New York: St Martin's Press, 1987, pp 630.

21. R. M. May, "HIV infection in heterosexuals", **Nature**, 25 February 1988, volume 331, pp 655-6.

22. P. Piot et al, "AIDS: An international perspective", **Science**, 5 February 1988, volume 235, pp 573-579.

23. H. Handsfield et al, "Association of anogenital ulcer disease with HIV infection in homosexual men", **Abstracts of the Third International Conference on AIDS**, Washington, D.C., June 1987 p 206; J.W. Curran et al, "Epidemiology of HIV infection in the United States", **Science**, 5

February 1988, volume 239, pp 610-6; J. Kreiss et al, "Role of sexually transmitted diseases in transmitting human immunodeficiency virus", **Genitourinary Médicine**, 1988, volume 64, pp 1-2.

24. P. Piot et al, op. cit.

25. W. Winkelstein et al, "Sexual practices and risk of infection by HIV: the San Francisco men's health study", **Journal of the American Medical Association**, 16 January 1987, volume 257, number 3, pp321-5 J. Levy et al, "Human immunodeficiency virus detected in bowel epithelium from patients with gastrointestinal symptoms", **Lancet**, 6 February 1988, pp 259-62

26. P. Piot et al, op. cit.

27. F. Plummer et al, **Abstracts of the Third International Conference on AIDS**, Washington DC, June 1987, p 6.

28. A. S. Latif et al, **Abstracts of the African Regional Conference on Sexually Transmitted Diseases,** Harare, Zimbabwe, June 1987, p 7.

29. P. Piot et al, op. cit; Cameron et al, **Abstracts of the Third International Conference on AIDS,** Washington DC, June 1987, p 25.

30. J. K. Kreiss et al, "Antibody to human t-lymphotropic virus type III in wives of hemophiliacs", **Annals of Internal Medicine**, May 1985, volume 102, number 5, pp 623-626; J. M. Jason et al, "HTLV- III/LAV antibody and immune status of household contacts and sexual partners of persons with hemophilia", **Journal of the American Medical Association**, 10 January 1986, volume 255, pp 212-215; **Morbidity and Mortality Weekly Report**, 11 September 1987, number 36, p 593; T. A. Peterman et al, Abstracts of the Second International Conference on AIDS, Paris, June 1986, p 107

31. World Health Organization, "Global WHO Strategy for the prevention and control of Acquired Immunodeficiency Sydnrom: Projected needs for 1986-1987", February 1986, p 4.

32. Report of the Third meeting of Participating Parties, WHO Special Programme on AIDS, Geneva, 27-28 April 1987, p 2.

33. R. Anderson and R. May, op. cit.

34. R. M. May and R. M. Anderson, "Transmission dynamics of HIV infection", **Nature**, volume 326, 12 March 1987, pp 137-142.

35. J. M. Mann et al, "Surveillance for AIDS in a Central Africa City", **Journal of the American Medical Association**, 20 June 1986, volume 255, number 23, pp 3255-59.

36. J. Desmyter et al, **Abstracts of the Second International Conference on AIDS**, Paris 1986 p 106.

37. N. Clumeck, "Epidemiological correlations between African AIDS and AIDS in Europe", **Infection,** 1986, volume 14, number 3, pp 97-9.

38. O.P. Arya and J.B. Lawson, op. cit.

39. J. K. Kreiss et al, "AIDS virus infection in Nairobi prostitutes", **New**

England Journal of Medicine, 13 February 1986, volume 314, number 7, pp 414-8.

40. P. Piot and A. Meheus, "Epidémiolie des maladies sexuellement transmissibles dans les pays en développement", **Ann. Soc. belge. Med. trop.**, 1983, volume 63, pp 87-110.

41. N. Nzilambi et al, "The Prevalence of Infection with HIV over a 10-year period in rural Zaire", **New England Journal of Medicine,** 1988, volume 315, number 5, pp 276-279.

42. R. Anderson and R. May, op. cit.

43. P.E.C. Manson-Bahr and F.I.C. Apted, **Manson's Tropical Diseases**, 18th Edition, London: Balliere-Tindall, 1982, pp 27-8.

44. T. C. Quinn et al, "Serologic and immunologic studies in patients with AIDS in North America and Africa", **Journal of the American Medical Association**, 15 May 1987, volume 257, number 19, p 2617.

45. L. J. Eales et al, "Association of different allelic forms of group specific component with susceptibility to and clinical manifestation of human immunodeciency virus", **Lancet**, 2 May 1987, p 999-1002.

46. L.J. Eales et al, **Lancet**, 30 May 1987, p 1268-69.

47. C. Bartholomew et al, **Abstracts of the Second International Symposium on AIDS and Associated Cancers in Africa**, October 1987, p 127.

48. F. I. D. Konotey-Ahulu, "Group specific component and HIV infection", **Lancet**, 30 May 1987, p 1267.

49. Interview, October 1987.

50. S.R. Friedman et al, "The AIDS epidemic among blacks and hispanics", report to be published in mid-1988 in the **Milbank Quarterly**, volume 65, number 2.

CHAPTER SEVEN: BLAME AND COUTER-BLAME

1. **Democrat and Chronicle**, Rochester, New York, 13 April 1987.

2. **Ghanaian Time**s, Accra, October 1987 quoted in the New York Times, 15 April 1987.

3. **Sunday Times**, Nairobi, 28 June 1987.

4. Interview, July 1987.

5. **The Economist**, 21 March 1987, p 59; **Le Monde**, Paris, 27 July 1987.

6. World Military and Social Expenditures, Washington, D.C., 1985; World Directory of Medical Schools, WHO, 1979; The World of Learning, The World of Learning, London: Europa Publications Ltd., 1986.

7. Interview, September 1987.

8. Interview, August 1987.

9. Interview, April 1988.

10. **Times**, London, 29 October 1986, part 3 of a series of articles on AIDS in Africa.

11. Ibid.

12. **La Gazette**, Yaoundé, 9 July 1987.

13. Ibid.

14. **New Vision**, Kampala, 10 February 1987.

15. **New York Times**, 19 November 1987.

16. **African Concord**, Lagos, 22 January 1987.

17. **La Gazette**, Yaoundé, 9 July 1987.

18. **Standard**, Nairobi, 14 January 1987.

19. Patrick Egbe, speaking at a seminar organised by the International Planned Parenthood Federation, Mbabane, Swaziland, August 1987.

20. **The Thunderbolt**, Marietta, Georgia, no date number 320.

21. J. Coombs, **The CDL Report**, Arabi, Louisiana, August 1987, issue 98, p 1.

22. **Evening News**, London, 21 September 1987.

23. J. Bouisset, **L'Action**, July/August 1987, pp 18-27.

24. K. Holness and K. Wong, **The AIDS Frame-up**, London: Black Health Workers and Patients' Group, March 1987, p 19.

25. Speech by Dr. Frances Cress Welsing at a conference on AIDS and Racism held in London, 20 November 1987; Dr. Welsing's views are elaborated in her pamphlet "The Cress Theory of Color, Confrontation and Racism (White Supremacy)", privately published, 1970, 15pp.

26. K. Holness and K. Wong, op cit; Don Edwards, executive director of the US National Minority AIDS Council, notes that minority group discussion on AIDS sometimes includes references to Tuskegee. The name Tuskegee has become symbolic of racial bias in US medicine, though he himself thinks that the parallel between what happened with the Tuskegee experiment and what is happening now with AIDS among minorities is inexact.

27. J. H. Jones, **Bad Blood**, New York: The Free Press, 1981, 272pp.

28. A. Davis, Women, **Race and Class**, London: The Women's Press, 1981, p 219.

29. **Time**, 6 July 1987, p 53.

30. Interview, February 1988.

31. Interview, October 1987. This physician asked that his name not be used.

32. **Times of Zambia**, Lusaka, 29 August 1987.

33. **Newswatch**, Lagos, 30 March, 1987.

34. Interview, November 1987.

35. Interview, December 1987.

36. Interview, August 1987.

37. Interview with Peter Fraenkel, February 1988.

38. **Monthly Life**, Lagos, May 1987.

39. Ibid.

40. Interview, August 1987.

41. Interview, December 1987.

42. Interview, December 1987.

43. Interview, August 1987.

44. Hilary Ng'weno, "AIDS in Africa: A racist taint", **Newsweek**, 23 March 1987, p 4.

45. Interview, October 1987.

46. **Kenya Times**, Nairobi, 4 December 1986.

47. **Sunday Nation**, Nairobi, 14 December 1986.

48. **Daily Nation**, Nairobi, 11 June 1987.

49. **Sunday Times of Zambia,** Lusaka, 21 December 1986.

50. **New Scientis**t, London, 27 November 1986, p 15.

51. F. I. Konotey-Ahulu, "AIDS in Africa: Misinformationn and Disinformation", **Lancet**, 25 July 1987, pp 206-207

52. R. C. Chirimuuta and R. J. Chirimuuta, **AIDS, Africa and Racism**, Bretby, Derbyshire: R.C. Chirimuuta, 1987, p 85.

53. **SIDA et tiers monde**, ENDA-Panos, Dakar, April 1987, 140pp.

54. **Sunday Times of Zambia**, Lusaka, 30 November 1986.

55. **Bangkok Post**, 25 January 1987.

56. **Herald**, Harare, 26 November 1987.

CHAPTER EIGHT WHO PAYS THE PRICE OF BLAME

1. Interview conducted by Zambian journalist Dave Moyo, Lusaka, July, 1987.

2. **Kenya Times**, Nairobi, 26 May 1987.

3. Ibid.

4. **Sunday Star**, Johannesburg, 13 September 1987.

5. **Sunday Star**, Johannesburg, 26 July 1987.

6. Ibid.

7. **International Herald Tribune**, 5 March 1987.

8. **Le Monde**, Paris, 18 March 1987.

9. **Newsweek,** 31 August 1987, p. 7.

10. **Sunday Telegraph**, London, 21 September 1986.

11. **Times of Zambia**, Lusaka, 23 September 1986.

12. Report on the Ministry of Health Seminar on AIDS, 24-26 July 1986, University Teaching Hospital, Lusaka, unpublished, 5pp.

13. Information on Zambian tourist industry from Zambian journalist Dave Moyo.

14. From text of Zambian letter, 13 October 1987, written to a British researcher.

15. **Guardian,** London, 3 February 1987.

16. **Guardian**, London, 25 March 1987.

17. **International Herald Tribune**, 23 November 1985.

18. Information supplied by Kenyan journalist Dorothy Kweyu Munyakho, August 1987.

19. **Standard**, Nairobi, 7 February 1987.

20. Ibid.

21. **Guardian**, London, 14 January 1987.

22. **New African,** London, March 1987, p 25.

23. **Daily Nation**, Nairobi, 14 January 1987.

24. **The Independen**t, London, 14 February 1987.

25. Report to Panos by London **Guardian** Tokyo correspondent Lisa Martineau, July 1987.

26. Written report to Panos, August 1987.

27. **Islam**, August 1987, p 50.

28. **Washington Post,** 12 November 1987.

29. M. L. Tan, Report on first conference on AIDS in Asia, November 1987.

30. Personal communication, Brenda Stoltzfus, PREDO, Philippines.

31. **O Globo**, Rio de Janeiro, 16 September 1987.

32. Interview with Mexican health offical who preferred not to be named, September 1987.

CHAPTER NINE: DIFFERENT PEOPLE, DIFFERENT MESSAGES

1. Written report to Panos by Hikloch Ogola, 1 February 1988.

2. Interviews, July 1987.

3. P. Piot et al, "AIDS: an international perspective" **Science**, 5 February 1988, volume 239, pp 573-90.

4. E. N. Ngugi, "Reaching the hard to reach", Health Ministers' Conference, London, January 1988.

5. Personal communication, Brenda Stolzfus, May 1987.

6. S. Allen, unpublished study.

7. Interview, March 1987.

8. **New York Times**, 4 January 1988.

9. Interview, November 1987.

10. J.W. Curran et al, "Epidemiology of HIV infection and AIDS in the United States", **Science**, vol 239, pp 610-616.

11. National AIDS Network (ed.),**Recorders' Notes, CDC Conference on AIDS in Minority Populations in the United States**, 8-9 August 1987, p 27.

12. Interview, November 1987.

13. Interview, November 1987.

14. Interview, February 1988.

15. Interview, February 1988.

16. Interview, September 1987.

17. Interview, November 1987.

18. Interview, October 1987.

19. Interview, September 1987.

20. Interview, February 1988.

21. **Washington Post**, 28 December 1987.

22. Ibid.

23. Interview, November 1987.

24. Stephen B. Thomas, **Knowledge of and Attitudes Towards AIDS: A Survey of Inner-City Black Residents in Selected Public Housing Units, Black Churches and Black College Freshmen (preliminary results)**, Minority Health Research Laboratory (MHRL), Department of Health Education, University of Maryland, 11-12 November 1987, pp 17 and 4 (appendix).

25. **Chicago Sun Times**, 29 November 1987.

26. S.R. Friedman et al, **The AIDS Epidemic Among Blacks and Hispanics**, report to be published in mid-1988 in **The Milbank Quarterly**, vol 65, no 2.

27. Ibid, p 32.

28. Interview, October 1987.

29. Interview, November 1987.

30. Interview, November 1987.

31. Interview, November 1987.

32. Interview, November 1987.

33. Ibid.

34. Interview, November 1987.

35. **New York Times**, 17 November 1987.

36. Interview, November 1987.

37. Interview, November 1987.

FURTHER ACKNOWLEDGEMENTS

Many individuals and organisations, both in developing and developed countries, made valuable contributions to the book at various stages. Publication of *Blaming Others: Prejudice, race and worldwide AIDS* would not have been possible without their help, but space prevents mentioning all their names. The names of those who read and commented on drafts or parts of the book, or who were interviewed for it, or who provided documentary material, appear below. While it could not have been written without their generosity, the book does not necessarily express their views.

BELGIUM:
Ekanga Shungu, Journal *Tam Tam*.

BRAZIL:
Paulo Fatel, GAPA, Rio de Janeiro; Esther Habib, AIDS Programme, Hospital Emilio Ribas; Luiz Mott, Grupo Gay de Bahia; Dr Lair Rodrigues & Dr Pedro Chequer, Brazilian National AIDS Committee; Dr Paulo Roberto Teixeira, São Paulo.

COSTA RICA:
Dr Leonardo Mata, National AIDS Committee.

FRANCE:
Dr Patrick Silberstein, Sida'venture; Paul Webster, Correspondent for the London *Guardian*.

ISRAEL:
Joanna Yehiel.

IVORY COAST:
James Brooke, Correspondent for the *New York Times*.

INDONESIA:
Hanna Rambe, *Mutiara*.

JAPAN:
Lisa Martineau, Correspondent for the London *Guardian*.

KENYA:
Dr William Cameron; Dr Anzeze Makindu; Ndirangu Maina; Elizabeth Ngugi, Chief Nursing Officer; Hilary Ng'weno, *Weekly Review*; Elizabeth Obel & Dominic Walibengo, KENGO; Jimoh Omo-Fadaka, ANEN; Otula Owuor, *Kenya Times*; "Peter".

MEXICO:
Dr Jaime Sepulveda, Dr Jose Valdespino, Ministry of Health.

NETHERLANDS:
Dr Marjo Meijer, International Committee on Prostitute Rights;
Dr C.J. van Dam.

NORWAY:
Agnete Strom, Women's Front.

PHILIPPINES:
Gabriela women's group.

SENEGAL:
Jacques Bugnicourt, ENDA.

SOUTH AFRICA:
Alfred Machela, Rand Gay Organisation; Pat Sidley, *Weekly Mail*.

SWEDEN:
Anders Wijkman, Swedish Red Cross

SWITZERLAND:
Dr Michel Caraël, Sev Fluss, Bob Groce, Dr André Meheus, World
Health Organization.

THAILAND:
Empower; Somattra Troy.

TRINIDAD AND TOBAGO
Dr Farley Cleghorn, Dr Courtenay Bartholomew, CAREC.

UGANDA:
Dr Samuel Okware, National AIDS Control Committee; Dr Ruhakana
Rugunda, former Minister of Health; Dr David Serwadda, Dr N.
Sewankambo, Mulago Hospital.

UNITED KINGDOM:
Caroline Akehurst & David FitzSimons, Bureau of Hygiene and
Tropical Diseases; Dr Roy Anderson, Imperial College; Paul Boateng,
MP; Enver Carim; Peter Fraenkel, broadcaster; Karen Holness, Black
Health Workers and Patients Group; Tisa Hughes; Winston Hunte,
Black Community AIDS Team; Eddie Iroh, *African Guardian*
magazine; Dr Paul Nunn & Dr Kwesi Tsiquaye, London School of
Hygiene and Tropical Medicine; Nick Partridge & Jim Wilson,
Terrence Higgins Trust; Thompson Prentice, *The Times*.

UNITED STATES:
Priscilla Alexander & Gloria Lockett, Coyote; Leslie Atkinson,
Congressional Black Caucus Health Brain Trust; Bob Baxter, AIDS
Community Support Unit, New Jersey State Health Department
Division of Narcotic and Drug Abuse Control; Rev Charles Bean,
Minority AIDS Project; William Bogan & Dr Jane Delgado,
COSSMHO; Dr Wilson Carswell, Family Health International; Alex

Compagnet, Salud Inc; David Cueny, Comprehensive AIDS Program of Palm Beach County Inc; Clarisa del Prado; Dr Don des Jarlais, New York City Health Department; David Dinkins, Manhattan Borough President; Don Edwards, National Minority AIDS Council; Dr Lenora Fulani, New Alliance Party; Gilberto Gerald, National AIDS Network; Dr Wayne Greaves, Howard University Hospital, Washington DC; Ellen Hale, Gannett News Service; Blaine Harden, *Washington Post* correspondent, Nairobi; Rashidah Hassan, BEBASHI; Michael Helquist, Academy for Educational Development; Mike Hooper, National Coalition for Haitian Refugees; Dr Gertrude Hunter, National Council of Negro Women; Dr Rudolph Jackson, Medical Consultant to the CDC; Chris Jacques and Sunny Rumsey, New York City Dept of Health; Elizabeth Miller Kummerfeld, American Foundation for AIDS Research; Steve Lambesis, National Urban Coalition; Jacqueline Lee, Hunter College School of Health Services; Cheryl Little, Haitian Refugee Center; Donna Long, New York Urban League; Genevieve Lopez, Milagros AIDS Project; Evelyn Lowery, Southern Christian Leadership Conference; Dr Edward Morales Multi-cultural Inquiry and Research on AIDS; Janet Nassim, World Bank; Peng Ngin, Asian AIDS Project; Pat Norman; Henri Norris, Multi-cultural Alliance for Prevention of AIDS; Tim Offutt, Kupona Network; Arturo Olivas, Cara a Cara; Ed Pitt, National Urban League; Suki Ports, Center for Democratic Renewal; Dr Beny Primm, Presidential AIDS Commission; Ruth Rodrigues, Hispanic AIDS Forum; Victor Hinojosa, Instituto Familiar de La Raza; Marie St Cyr, Director, Haitian Coalition on AIDS; Dr Ron St John & Dr Fernando Zacarias, Pan American Health Organization; Larry Saxxon, San Francisco Black Coalition on AIDS; Ben Schatz, AIDS Civil Rights Project National Gay Rights Advocate; Althea Simmons, NAACP; Dr Roulette Smith, California; Jack Stein, Health Education Resource Organization; Brenda Stolzfus; Jerl Surratt, Lambda Legal Defense and Education Fund; Dr Charles Symington, National Medical Association; Katy Taylor, New York City Commission on Human Rights AIDS Discrimination Unit; Dr Stephen Thomas, Department of Health Education at the University of Maryland; Barbara Turk; Paula Van Ness, National AIDS Information Program, Centers for Disease Control; George Marshall Worthington, New York.

Zaire
Zambia

risk grp → origin of dz → blamed,
                            stigmatized →

                                                    not
                    Ø = risk   solve
                                                    the
                        counter blame →   problem

              * not all classified
                 as risk grp
                 have risk

              * non-risk grp is
                 not ∅ risk
vs risk activity
                    ~ not caused by
              local clx but
              global capitalism & clx